INTUITION

INTUITION

Access your inner wisdom • Trust your instincts • Find your path

AMISHA GHADIALI

Senior Editor Emma Hill
Project Art Editor Alison Gardner
Senior Designer Barbara Zuniga
Managing Editor Dawn Henderson
Managing Art Editor Marianne Markham
Editorial Assistant Kiron Gill
Production Editor David Almond
Production Controller Rebecca Parton
Senior Jacket Designer Nicola Powling
Jacket Co-ordinator Lucy Philpott
Art Director Maxine Pedliham
Publishing Director Mary-Clare Jerram,
Katie Cowan

Illustrator Eiko Ojala,
additional illustrations Alison Gardner

First published in Great Britain
in 2020 by Dorling Kindersley Limited
DK, One Embassy Gardens,
8 Viaduct Gardens, London, SW11 7BW

For the curious

www.dk.com

CONTENTS

FOREWORD

Living from my intuition has made me feel more alive, present, and that I am "myself". I have discovered deeper layers of freedom, joy, and flow. I know you can experience this too. The path here for me wasn't always smooth, from relying too much on other people's guidance to near-death experiences to becoming an intuitive therapist. I had to keep opening myself up and look at everything with fresh eyes. I had to let myself do or say things that I would have at some stage thought impossible. I had to trust.

As my relationship with my inner world developed, I found wholeness and a sense of clarity that had been missing during the years I didn't listen. It has been an extraordinary adventure. Throughout my life I have been deeply exploring two questions. How can I live the most full and true version of myself? And how can we co-create a beautiful future? I believe that intuition is the key to

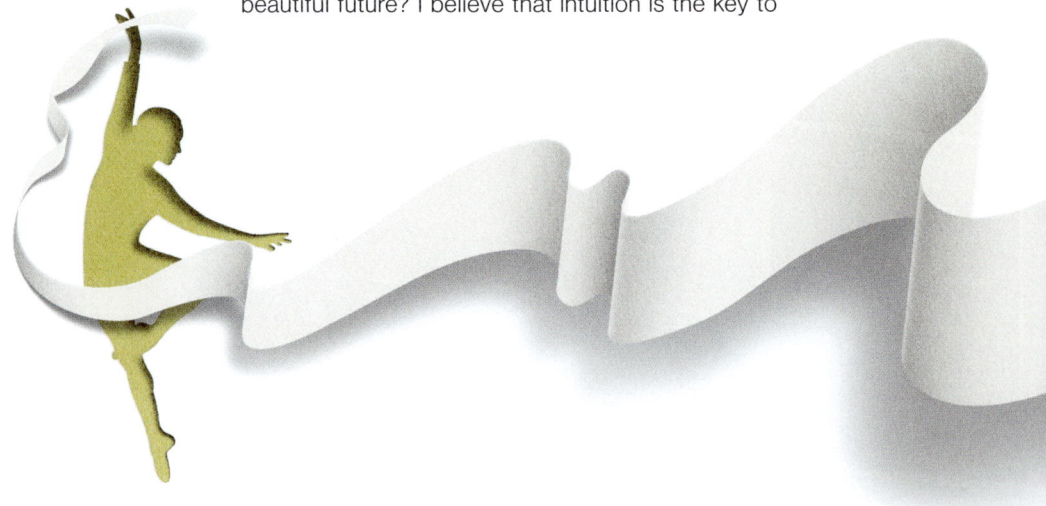

both. It feels to me that unlearning our mistrust of it, and fully embodying our inner wisdom is the most important skill of this time. As we learn to live with more uncertainty and as technology advances, that which makes us uniquely human feels even more significant.

I see how needed our intuition is, not just for our personal happiness but also for our collective healing. I believe that our intuition is one of the most precious and untapped resources we have. And it moves me to imagine what could happen if we all started to live from this potential.

In this book I share the information, teachings, and practices that I have found most useful in embodying my inner wisdom, and living an intuitive life. It comes from many years of studying and transformational experiences. I hope this inspires you and that you discover the most beautiful things about yourself.

Imisha Ghadiali

THE LOST ART OF INTUITION

WHAT IS INTUITION?

Intuition is our ability to know something instinctively without having to discover it or rationalize it intellectually – a deep sense of knowing without an analytical process. You can't explain to anyone why – you don't have statistics or research to back up your perspective. You just know.

This is a capacity that absolutely everyone has; you were born with it. You use your intuition every day without thinking about it, whenever you do something out of your usual habit. It's innate in you as a human being, but like everything it needs to be developed and honed as a skill. The more you use it, the stronger and more attuned it becomes. We are all intuitive as children, but many of us disconnect from our intuition in our teen years, as we try to make sense of the world and find our place in it. If you feel disconnected from this part of you, know that intuition is not a new thing to develop, but something to uncover and enhance.

Intuition is not in competition with our rational mind, it's just another part of ourselves that we use all the time, but often in a limited unconscious way. Your rational mind and your intuitive sense can work together; this is when the real power of your intelligence comes to life. By developing your intuition and giving it the kudos it deserves, you can open up to greater possibility, expansiveness, and more flow in every area of your life.

THAT GUT FEELING

Have you ever had a gut feeling? You can't explain why but you get a sense that you need to cancel a trip, call somebody right away, or go to a certain place. And when you do, you either stopped something terrible from happening or you found a life-changing opportunity such as a new job or relationship. Did you ever feel inspired to take a longer journey to work than your usual route and found out that you avoided an accident or bumped into somebody you haven't seen for ages? Have you ever had a feeling about a person the moment you met them – that you could really trust them, and they turned out to be a lifelong friend? Or when you saw a house, you just knew it was the right one for you? What about a sense that you needed to go into your child's bedroom just in time to catch something that was about to fall on them? Or to stop by an elderly relative's house just after they had fallen? With a quiet, still, inner voice guiding you, you knew you were in the right place at the right time.

66 99

INTUITION IS SEEN BY MANY AS THE HIGHEST FORM OF INTELLIGENCE

When you get that feeling or you hear that inner voice guiding you, this is your intuition. It's not magic; it's informed by your past experiences, the data you have collected through life, and an unconscious understanding of what is the most aligned way forward for you. It's connected to a collective intelligence we can all access. It's a felt sense and a clear perception.

YOUR INTUITIVE VOICE

The way your intuition speaks to you is as unique as you are. Your intuition can be felt in different ways; for some it's a voice or melodies that you hear, for others it's vivid dreams that you have, for some a strong sensation can be felt in your body, for others it's signs that you see in your environment.

We all have a survival-based instinct that keeps us safe. Everyone can access this without thinking – it doesn't require any training, is natural, and keeps you out of danger in a very obvious way. Intuition becomes more nuanced when it's the type that conveys insight for your life and your choices. This guidance only makes sense for you, as it's based on your soul's purpose and living a fulfilling and beautiful life that is unique to you. This cannot be validated by anyone else. It is something you have to cultivate in yourself.

For those of a more rational mindset, you will learn to work through barriers, mental roadblocks, and your resistance – and to open up to experiences that feel uncomfortable or strange based on your current perceptions. For those of you who are more empathic or highly sensitive and are used to picking up on a lot of intuitive information, you will have to learn how to discern what is yours and to trust yourself.

Your personal GPS

The word intuition comes from the Latin word intueri, which means "to contemplate" or "to look within". To be able to hear the guidance you receive, and to take action on it, you need to really know your Self and have healthy self-esteem. You have to appreciate yourself and the wisdom that you carry.

Consider your intuition as your "inner-tuition" where the teacher is your own highest truth. We are always in a process of growth and there is a part of us that exists in a state of true knowing. Our intuition connects us to this knowing, so we are sure of which steps to take next. For some of you, this will be new as you forge a relationship with your inner world, and for others it will serve as a reminder, or give you permission to embrace something you already know but can now put into action and trust, fully.

Your intuition can guide you to make wise decisions that bring more joy, love, and presence into your life. Choices that take you away from a need to control and limit everything and instead open up your life to creativity, adventure, and insight. Think of it as your GPS for your soul.

Your life is made up of a series of decisions. Of course there are the big decisions that you may agonize over, such as whether to take that job, or move to another country.

" "

LIFE IS MADE UP OF A SERIES OF DECISIONS

However, you are making small decisions every day that have a big impact on your life – whether you walk down one street or another, if you are late or early for that meeting, what to wear today, or whether to go to that party or not. These are all decisions that you either make out of habit or fear, or from your intuition. What would transform in your life if you were able to make all these decisions from this clear, uplifted, and expansive place, without having to analyse or agonize over them, or just do what you have always done? What would happen if you let your intuition guide you?

WHY HAVE WE LOST OUR INTUITION?

We live in a rational-lensed society, where the focus is on seeing the surface level of reality and being able to explain and prove everything as true or false – while also disregarding the unseen and unexplainable. In human development, the rational part of our brain evolved later than our instinct, yet more emphasis is put on rational thought processes through our education systems and dominant culture.

In ancient cultures, intuition was a central part of life. It goes back as far as hunters and gatherers, who used their intuition to find food and stay safe. There are stories of women from Native American tribal cultures all coming together when they were menstruating – a time when women are known to be more intuitive, sensitive, and connected to collective wisdom. They would all sleep in a circle with their heads together, and dream a collective dream that would tell the men where the buffalo were, so the tribe could eat. In these cultures the intuitive and the rational world danced together as a way of life.

THE DE-VALUING OF INTUITION

There are many global historical events, from witch-hunts to colonialism, that have forced intuition underground. Cultures all over the world that valued intuition and passed down intelligent techniques and wisdom for survival and thriving were endangered, murdered, and enslaved.

This has had a deep impact on our global culture. Many of the words associated with living an intuitive life have become derogative, such as "loon" to denote a crazy person, when it really means living in tune with the moon's cycles, which all human beings are affected by. This is information we all take in, through our ancestral and cultural conditioning. So much so that the mention of the word witches here may have put you off reading more of this book, as you possibly dismissed it as strange, or woo woo. Pay attention, as that is how strong the imprinting is that separates us from our intuitive wisdom.

Suppression of the feminine

Our intuition and other related receptive qualities, such as listening and nurturing, are considered to be our "feminine" qualities. The fear and undermining of the feminine has led to a culture that is focused on the action-based masculine qualities of doing, rationalizing, and fixing. Whether you identify as a man, woman, or gender neutral, you have within you both masculine and feminine aspects. These are deep archetypal traits that complement each other, as the Chinese symbol of the Yin and the Yang shows. If you are in balance, you will have access to both these sets of skills, and they can work together in coherence.

Intuition versus capitalism

There are indigenous cultures around the world where intuition is still a part of daily life, such as tribal cultures in the Amazon. Many of these indigenous tribes have powerful initiations and their people are trained to live intuitively and protect the rainforests. They have healers and shamans that can tune in to people's feelings and suffering all around the globe. They have premonitions about what is going to happen so they can prepare. This is also true of the yogis in India, and other spiritual cultures across the world.

In Asia, ancient wisdom and spiritual traditions sit side by side with the modern way of life. In India, for example, it is very normal to have astrology readings for all major business and life decisions. In Bali there are ceremonies and rituals every day. In Japan there are special days in the calendar where you would launch a business or get married. In China, it is common to have fortune-tellers present in business meetings. There is a counterculture in the West inspired by these Eastern and indigenous ways. However, as few parts of the world are untouched by global capitalism, there is often a tension between generations, economic progress, or the demands of both ways of life.

" "

IN ASIA, ANCIENT WISDOM AND SPIRITUAL TRADITIONS SIT SIDE BY SIDE WITH THE MODERN WAY OF LIFE

INTUITION IN THE MODERN WORLD

Our global society and education system prepare us to be industrial workers and consumers so we feed the system. If we were all empowered in our intuition and following our soul's purpose we would be unlikely to orient our lives around being employable, paying off debt, and keeping up with the latest trends. So we are entrained to be "followers" on social media, and live lifestyles that have our autonomic nervous systems in constant "fight or flight" mode – your body's natural response when you feel you are in danger.

Personal and collective trauma

There is enormous personal and collective trauma that nobody is immune from. We live in a world where high levels of depression, anxiety, stress, and addictions are normalized. In addition, we have all been affected by the systems of oppression we live within, including patriarchy, neoliberalism, and racism.

It can be difficult to find space to get into a calm state, where your body can perform its natural intelligent healing and you can easily make intuitive decisions. Many of us are scared to trust our intuition and are reluctant to believe it is real. Or we feel too stressed out and frazzled – we are living life on a hamster wheel rather than getting out of the cage. We can become imprisoned in our mind, yet it's the only prison that has no walls. We're free to walk out at any moment. The door is there, and intuition is the key to open it.

" "

MANY OF US ARE SCARED TO TRUST OUR INTUITION

HOW TO LIVE
AN INTUITIVE LIFE

Intuition is a powerful untapped aspect of our human potential, an excellent resource that is ready to be proudly brought into use, not just for our personal happiness but also for our collective future.

TODAY'S VISIONARIES

Intuition is a key invisible force in today's world. Many of society's essential professions rely on intuition – for emergency service workers such as firefighters and paramedics, they have extensive training but their snap decisions are a matter of life or death. They learn to trust their hunches, follow their intuition, and often don't have the luxury of time to reason or analyse their decisions.

Our creatives live through their intuition; it guides musicians, artists, and writers on where to stroke the paintbrush, or what to write on the page. Many musicians talk about hearing the songs from their inner voice, the lyrics and chords fully formed. Several high-profile people attribute their success to their intuition, such as tech-founder billionaires and CEOs. It's often a marker of those who are pushing boundaries and doing something visionary that hasn't been done before. Visionaries are edgewalkers who walk between worlds. These futurists, leaders, and shamans

" "

IF YOU ARE A VISIONARY YOU SEE CONNECTIONS BETWEEN SEEMINGLY UNRELATED THINGS, AND MAKE BOLD DECISIONS.

shape the world we live in – they think "outside of the box", see connections between seemingly unrelated things, and make bold decisions. How do they know what to do? Where do they get their confidence from to take big risks and bring their visions into the world? To bring healing and innovation? How do they create future culture? They have soul purpose, integrity, and are self-aware. They trust their intuition.

Where to begin

In this book we explore how to create a deep relationship with your own intuition, be open to unseen worlds, and understand your potential. This is an incredible time to be alive, where we all have permission to openly live from our intuition. In the age of fake news and so many conflicting narratives, it's more important than ever to be able to listen to your intuition to discern what is happening on a collective level and what is right for you. Your intuition will guide you to knowing yourself and creating a life that is perfect for you and your deeper purpose.

THE
PRINCIPLES
OF INTUITION

CREATE SPACE

We live in a culture that glorifies being busy, and we have many pressures on us at all times. To build a stronger relationship with your intuition, you first need to carve out space to enable inner shifts and listen to your own wisdom. This could be a literal space in your house or place of work, time as space, or precious headspace.

You may have a demanding work, family, or social life and find it hard to take time for yourself. It's easy to fill every moment with some commitment or pressure. You might have a sense that taking time for yourself is a luxury. Many of us are scared to have space to be alone and truly feel and be with ourselves because it's such unexplored territory. Whatever

" "

IN ORDER TO LISTEN TO THE VOICE OF KNOWING INSIDE OF YOU, YOU NEED TO SLOW DOWN

your circumstances, in order to listen to the voice of knowing inside of you, to be able to give to yourself in a conscious way, you need to slow down. If you don't leave space, nothing outside of what you have planned can happen. You are constantly reacting to life, rather than creating it. The phone won't suddenly stop beeping, and other people will never stop needing more from you – only you have the power to set the boundaries that you need in order to create space.

Get some headspace

Where in your diary can you make space, let go of things, and create more time for you? It can start with just ten minutes a day, and then something very potent happens when you can give yourself whole evenings or chunks of the weekend. Time is precious, and it can be so easy to give it away to things that don't fulfil you, like all those hours clicking aimlessly through social media. What in your life is unnecessary and taking up space? Where are you over-giving? Outside of your main responsibilities such as family and work, what in your diary doesn't give you pleasure?

Do you have obligations that you feel you have to or "should" do? If there is a "should" in there, you already know it's not something that's truly aligned. When you say "should", consider who you are listening to. If you "should" do something, is that according to the values you grew up with, the society you are living in, or the expectations of somebody else? "Should" never comes directly from you and your true values. From that authentic place there is possibility, such as "I could", or there is desire, such as "I want", or there is taking responsibility such as "I need" – and then there is will. One way to create more space is to ban the word "should" entirely. Any "shouldness" you have in your head directly contradicts intuition because it sits above the moment of now, twisting it to places it may not naturally want to move. To live an inspired, intuitive life is to have deep purpose and meaning behind and through everything that we do.

Curate your space

The physical space you spend time in has a deep impact on how you feel and the wisdom you can hear. Have you ever been somewhere you immediately felt uplifted and inspired? Or on the opposite side, sat in a space where you felt lazy and down? Your home doesn't have to be picture-perfect. But creating space that is clear and free of clutter can be so supportive of your relationship with your intuition. Clutter creates chaos and disorder – and it can cause stress, lack of focus, and make your headspace noisy and draining. A simple rule you can apply to everything you own is that you either love it, use it regularly, or need it.

Having a cluttered space can come from avoidance, perfectionism, indecisiveness, or sheer overwhelm. How can you make the spaces that you use most often inspiring, open, and functional? This can mean clearing the clutter from anywhere you regularly spend time such as your desk, your bedroom, your car, or your whole living space. Everyone has a different tolerance level around clutter and the energy of a space, yet very few people feel uncomfortable or uninspired in a beautifully designed and organized space where thought has gone into the primary activities that will take place there. Small things such as where the furniture goes, or bringing in specific plants to bring life to your space, or putting things into an attractive box rather than a pile can make a big difference to how spacious and inspired you feel.

Step away from technology

Yes it's amazing that we have access to the whole world at our fingertips, but the combination of the electromagnetic frequencies from all our technology, and the fact that it means there is always more information coming in, can make it harder to find clear space. We have never been as aware of so many people, places, and world events as we are now. We have a constant stream of information coming in from social media, TV, and advertising that we then need to digest. Each of these is leaving impressions in our mind and energy field, taking up space. With your phone, you are always on – often somebody texts you getting straight into a need or an emotion without checking if you are open to it first; you receive emails asking you to do things, news sources worrying you about conflicts and issues in the world, and so it goes on. Most people sleep with

their phones right next to their heads, and the last thing they do at night and the first thing they do in the morning is to scroll through it. This means that this precious time when preparing for sleep and greeting the new day is immediately filled up with things outside of yourself. This is often a time when our intuition is strongest, and if you are busy taking in new, unimportant information on social media, then you miss it. How would it feel to set up the technology in your house so that it supports you but doesn't control you?

Interrogate your habits

It's easy to pick up habits along the way that mean you never have any space. For example, coming home from work and switching on the TV. There's nothing wrong with watching a show that you love and enjoy, but often the act of sitting on the couch and watching the screen becomes so familiar that it doesn't matter if you are really enjoying what you consume. In fact the game can become finding the most interesting thing that is available to watch, rather than considering how you would really most like to spend your evening. Then you find what started out as watching a great show has evolved into numbing out in front of the television every night no matter what is on. And there is no space to do some of the other things you had wanted to do, like read that book or call that friend. Toxic relationships can be similar to this; you make a concession once or twice to help somebody out, and then before you know it that relationship is taking over your space and leaving you drained. It's easy to forget that you are in control of your own life, and everything you do and consume. When your intuition is blocked, you can fall into being a victim of circumstances, unable to see another way to create your life. But this wisdom is always there waiting to talk to you and show you another way.

How many things in your life have become habits that no longer serve you? And where can you find more space for you, to welcome in a deeper and more wonderful relationship with yourself, and to invite your intuition to guide you to live a fulfilling and beautiful life?

For practices that will help you to create space see pages 80–87

" "

THE PHYSICAL SPACE YOU SPEND TIME IN HAS A DEEP IMPACT ON HOW YOU FEEL AND THE WISDOM YOU CAN HEAR

BE
OPEN

You may be new to using your intuition, or at least to using it consciously. Cultivating an attitude of openness and curiosity is key to being ready to receive new wisdom and expand in all areas of your life.

Living life open to new possibilities and new realities, and being comfortable with the unknown, can be difficult. You are strongly wired to take in the culture around you and to live in your habits and routines. This includes how you think as well as what you do. Have you ever heard that you are the sum of the five people you spend the most time with? This is because we are all influenced by our environments and the cultural norms that surround us. As we are made up of so much possibility – more than we can embody in a moment – we align to those around us. When we lived in tribes, we had to fit in as part of the pack

" "

AN INTUITIVE PERSON IS SIMPLY EMBRACING POSSIBILITY

in order to survive. Those who didn't found themselves cast out into the wilderness and it was a matter of life or death. Even though today you won't be roaming the jungle trying to find food alone, your natural human response is still to follow the pack and to fit in with those around you. Remember, we live in a culture that doesn't value intuition (yet). It is often judged as weird or woo woo, and quite frankly disrespected. However, an intuitive person is simply embracing possibility. Judgment comes from patterns of fear and misery. It's important to be light-hearted when it comes to judgement you receive and that which you apply to yourself. There is nothing to fear by unleashing your intuition.

We are both influenced and influencers; in a reactive, fearful space we are highly swayed by our environment and people in our lives. When we are in a creative state, we have the power to choose our thoughts and actions, to open up more possibilities both for ourselves and those around us.

The lens of our conditioning

We are conditioned by our experiences in life, our family's values and story, the culture of our workplace, the school that we went to, the magazines that we read, and so on. All of this information enters into our subconscious and affects how we think, feel, and act. Your subconscious mind is all the information you have stored that you are not fully aware of. What is interesting about this is that even if you put in a lot of effort to develop certain patterns or behaviours, your core thoughts come from the beliefs you received as a child.

Between the third trimester in your mother's womb and the age of seven, you are at your most sponge-like – you are learning and taking in everything that you are exposed to. This means that at a young age you can learn new skills easily; everything from walking and how to tie your shoelaces, to speaking different languages and riding a bike. Until the age of seven, your brain is in a theta brainwave state, which means there is no filter. Your consciousness isn't yet able to evaluate the data it is receiving, to choose if you want to store it or not. This is important because as an adult, 95 per cent of your thoughts come from your subconscious and 75 per cent of these are often limiting, self-sabotaging beliefs. Only 5 per cent of your thoughts come from the conscious mind that you cultivate as an adult. This can keep you in a loop where you are living out your past, and in particular your childhood, constantly. If you use this lens of awareness to look around at people you know well, such as your loved ones, colleagues, or friends, it's not difficult to see what they were like as a child.

Embrace the unknown

You have around 60,000 thoughts a day. On average 95 per cent are the same as the ones you had yesterday. For many people, the majority of these are negative thoughts coming from limiting beliefs in the subconscious, unless you have done deep work to clear such beliefs or have a mindset that is predominantly positive. This explains why being open to new ideas and new ways of being can be difficult. It can be easy to get stuck in your ways and give up when trying new things.

The exciting part is that with some attention and awareness, you are able to reprogram your subconscious. Therapies like energy healing and hypnosis can be great for this as they take you out of your conscious mind into your subconscious and allow you to change the information you have stored. You can alter the way you think and open yourself up to new thought patterns and therefore new experiences. This means that you can start the process today to open up to your intuitive nature, even if this is something that you have never paid any attention to in the past, or understood, or perhaps even believed in.

Your brain is constantly evolving and is shaped by your experiences. There is a paradox here, in that you can both get stuck in repetitive patterns and you can train your brain to open up new neural pathways. Your brain has neuroplasticity, which means it is able to change through what you experience and as you learn and adapt. This is the muscle building part of your brain – just like with your body, what you use often becomes stronger and what you don't use becomes weak. As you age, your brain becomes less plastic, but this is often because you are not as open to changes. If you keep yourself receptive to new experiences, new possibilities, and new skills you are keeping this plasticity alive. With each repetition of a new thought or emotion or pattern, you reinforce a neural pathway, which in turn creates a new way of being.

The science of epigenetics

It's helpful to know that even when it comes to reprogramming your subconscious or healing disease there is science that shows this is possible. It was previously believed that your health was pre-determined solely by your heredity – if everyone in your family has had heart disease then you will too. The science of epigenetics has shown that this is not necessarily true – that your body, as in your DNA that determines your health and your experience of life, is impacted by your mind's interpretation of what is going on as well as environmental factors. For example, if you have a belief that at the age of 50 you will get heart disease like your father did, then you are programming that to occur. This is mainly your subconscious mind at work, not the conscious parts of your brain – but even so, you can bring your conscious mind to bear on the programming, and change it. Your 50 trillion body cells all receive information from your mind, and studies have shown that it is possible to grow physical muscle just by imagining yourself doing a workout every day. Participants visualized themselves doing a set of physical exercises and the results showed up as muscle on their bodies.

The power of an open mind

The more you are able to take a creative and playful attitude to life, and let your imagination run wild, the more miracles, and wild and beautiful experiences you can create. When you know this, it is greatly empowering as you realize you don't have to be a victim of what you have experienced in the past, what has happened to your family, your current circumstances, or even what is happening in the place where you live. You no longer have to limit yourself, or believe those around you who restrict your reality. Your present moment no longer has to be defined by your past. You're bringing your whole self into this very moment.

It's really quite something! You are able to influence your thoughts, emotions, beliefs, and experiences. And then in turn you are able to receive deep wisdom that you might have passed off before as strange or weird. You'll possibly find that by delving into this deeper reality you'll automatically attract people doing the same; people who support your expansion. Life has ways of bringing us together.

When you embrace the unknown and try new things or new perspectives, you activate the right side of your brain and it quietens the rational mind. By being open and curious and allowing yourself to keep learning, and by letting your intuition guide you, you can become who you really are – without all the baggage you have been carrying – and from that place create a life of the highest possibilities, a healthy body, a clear and focused mind, and the ability to bring new ideas, paradigm shifts, and collective healing to the planet. Let your life be an extraordinary adventure!

For practices that will encourage you to be open see pages 88–95

EMBODY

Your intuition speaks to you through your whole body. In fact Yogic philosophy makes no distinction between the body and the mind as it is all interconnected. Understanding yourself as a "bodymind" means you can bring awareness, empowerment, freedom, and full body listening into your life.

Society focuses so much on the rational mind that we are trained to think our way through life. In addition, our lifestyles have become very sedentary; we're often crouched over a computer for hours, eating processed foods and normalizing addictions to stress, sugar, caffeine, and alcohol. Bringing movement, awareness, and stillness into your whole body opens up its potential and brings you into embodiment.

Emotions and trauma in the bodymind

When you have awareness in your whole body, your thinking mind becomes part of a symphony of neurons, sensations, and signals through which you receive information and give information. You are doing this all the time anyway, you just might not be doing it consciously. For example, your body language can express what you are thinking and feeling without you having to say anything.

Our past experiences are stored in the body. All emotions and trauma that haven't been digested and processed become part of our bodymind, and then in turn influence how we feel, what we think, and what we do. Our traumas – our wounds – form and build on whatever is in our subconscious.

An emotion in its true form, as energy in motion, only lasts 90 seconds. The rest of our experience of that emotion is to do with our wounds and the stories we tell ourselves. Trauma is something that all of us have experienced, especially in childhood. It's often said it takes a village to raise a child, and most of us didn't have a whole village, with multiple safe parental figures, and so all our needs weren't met. As well as survival needs such as food and a place to sleep, we have other psychological needs that include secure attachment – so you feel safe and that you belong – and acceptance of your authentic self, so you don't have to pretend to be somebody else, act out, or hold back. Even if you came from a very loving, nurturing home, you will have picked up on some cultural or ancestral trauma, or had traumatic experiences at school. And there is the physical trauma that you might get from a car accident or a sports injury, and the adult emotional trauma from experiences like relationship breakups or judgments. This trauma affects the quality of your intuition as your pain could be directing you to make certain decisions arising from difficult emotions such as fear, anger, shame, guilt, or sadness. In some situations your trauma means that you are "not in your body" – in order to not feel the pain, you have dissociated from your body so you can't feel the weight of the trauma. This is a defence or coping mechanism. Not only does it affect your decisions but it can lead to illness as well, colouring the lens through which you see life. When the bodymind becomes unbearably full with unresolved energy, we squeeze our soul out and then live in a perpetual cycle of wanting to make ourselves feel better, often by numbing out through destructive and addictive behaviour.

The intelligence of your bodymind
Some strong trauma needs to be worked out over time with experienced bodyworkers such as osteopaths or with trauma-informed therapists. Other trauma you can release through bodily movement and awareness – such as yoga, five rhythms dancing, and breathwork. The intelligence of your bodymind means that if you give it time and space to heal by coming into "rest and digest" – your parasympathetic nervous system – it can heal itself and in turn bring more aliveness to every cell. For example in yoga, through the series of poses and working with your breath, you start to feel and pay attention to parts of your body that you haven't before, such as your little toe, which you'd normally only notice if you stubbed it, or your shoulder, which would only come to mind if you had an injury. When you bring your whole bodymind "online" you can receive the wisdom that it holds. There is a clarity that you feel in your bodymind, as you get connected to your embodied power. In this state

> **" "**
>
> **BRINGING MOVEMENT, AWARENESS, AND STILLNESS INTO YOUR WHOLE BODY OPENS UP ITS POTENTIAL AND BRINGS YOU INTO EMBODIMENT**

you can receive understanding of where your body is in dis-ease before an illness starts, and what you need to do about it. By strengthening every part of your bodymind, you release the potency you hold in each of these parts too. You are then able to receive a full bodymind "yes" – where you feel that something is right for you in your whole body, not just in your mind or your gut.

The heart brain

Science has shown that there is a "second brain" in our hearts with around 40,000 sensory neurites that communicate with the brain – that we have heart intelligence. The heart sends more information to the brain than the brain sends to the heart. Your brain responds to these signals from the heart that influence emotional processing, attention, perception, memory, and problem-solving. It's possible to measure your heart rate variability, which shows the level of coherence your heart is in and how your nervous system is functioning.

Combined with the science, many spiritual and wisdom traditions have focused on the heart, from the ancient Egyptians who saw it as the centre of life and wisdom to the ancient Greeks who regarded it as the centre of the soul. Often we are told to live from our hearts or speak from the heart. For many people, the inner voice feels like it comes from the heart – wisdom and guidance that is most aligned to how you feel. It is said that the hardest journey is from the head to the heart, but you just need to bring them into alignment. When you have a clear intention, you have brain coherence, and when you have emotions that elevate you such as gratitude, love, compassion, joy, and acceptance, you have heart coherence. This in turn fires off the parts of your brain that increase energy, creativity, and intuition. When you access your heart intelligence you are able to achieve higher levels of awareness and wholeness.

The gut brain

Your third brain is in the gut. We contain trillions of bacteria, fungi, viruses, and other microbes, called microbiome – most of this is in our gut and acts as our body's operating system. This consists of 90 per cent of the cells in our bodies and over 99 per cent of the DNA. Your microbiome communicates directly with the brain through a system of 100 million nerve cells in the lining of your gut. This affects how you feel emotionally as well as physically, and even what you think. More than 90 per cent of your serotonin and 50 per cent of your dopamine come from your gut. These neurotransmitters affect how you feel, how you sleep, as well as your memory and libido. This is where the phrase "you are what you eat" comes from. In addition to the nutritional value of what you eat and how this powers your body, what you consume also influences your thoughts and therefore the decisions you make.

Full body listening

When you are in alignment you are able to receive a full body "yes" which is a green light! This simply means that your head (thinking), heart (feeling), and gut (knowing) are all in alignment, and that you have coherence in your physical, emotional, and energetic body. This affects the hormones and chemicals that fire off as well as what you are capable of doing. If you see yourself holistically, you can hear the wisdom of your whole bodymind. There is an emphasis in society on perfectionism or presenting ourselves in a certain way, rather than loving how amazing and unique

and weird we each are. You have very sophisticated self-mending ways of dealing with hurt, toxins, and disease. By coming into a loving relationship with your whole body, and therefore your whole self, you invite this rebalance to take place. A healthy, happy bodymind coupled with self-acceptance leads to clear decisions and decisive action.

For practices to help bring you into embodiment see pages 96–113

BE
STILL

Stillness is such a powerful skill in our time. So much arises when you allow yourself to just be. When you let go of the doing and the thinking and feel into the miracle that is you, simply as you are right now, intuition rises.

Silence and stillness can be scary for many people in the modern world. How much time have you honestly spent not moving or doing anything or adding any new inputs into your world? When you develop a loving relationship with yourself, and connect to your soul, spending quality alone time can be the most beautiful, revitalizing, and potent experience. When you can literally rest in your stillness, the voice of your intuition is at its strongest. This stillness includes getting good sleep and rest, as well as practices such as meditation and yoga nidra. Or simply sit in silence and ask yourself what are the motivating forces

" "

STILLNESS CREATES A GROUND OF BEING FROM WHICH YOU CAN LISTEN MORE DEEPLY

pushing you to be active? Most often it's our programming to be productive and it's this force that requires letting go. You were created by the universe and you are enough.

Mindfulness, heartfulness, and self-care

When you spend time still, you can hear the quality of your thoughts, and make the effort to bring more spaciousness into your mind. You can notice which thoughts or limiting beliefs are reoccurring – what has been bothering you. You can sit in deep contemplation about something that you have going on in your life and let your wisdom come. You can notice how you feel and what kind of self-care you need. Rather than seeing stillness as something to dread or as boring, you can understand it as sacred "you time" where you can deeply connect to yourself and process everything that may have been happening in your life and your inner world. You can reset yourself and your nervous system. You can achieve balance and harmony. New ideas and creative inspiration can come. Stillness creates a ground of being from which you can listen more deeply. You're ultimately becoming your own best friend.

The subtle body

As you spend time in stillness and quietness, you develop a stronger relationship with yourself and awareness of your subtle body. Through this you can feel your own vibration, or frequency of light. You have aura layers – an auric field of energy, of light vibration – around your physical body. Closer in towards your body, these layers get slower and more dense. In the yogic understanding of the subtle body, you have 72,000 nadis, which are conduits of energy and prana (lifeforce) – you can visualize them as rivers of light. There are three main ones: Ida (which starts at your left nostril and relates to the energy of the moon and the feminine); Pingala (which starts at your right nostril and relates to the energy of the sun and the masculine); and your central channel in the spinal cord, the Shushumna Nadi. This central channel connects your energy centres, also called your chakras as they are wheels of energy.

The chakras

There are seven widely known chakras, although there is much debate over whether the system that everyone has come to know is accurate. Either way, they give a map of energy in the body that is useful, especially when this is new to you. And don't worry about understanding every aspect first – you'll find that, as your journey unfolds, you'll be drawn to understanding each aspect as it's shown to you. It's not something to remember, but something to be. Each chakra represents a different function in your emotional, spiritual, and physical health. They receive, assimilate, and express our vital life energy. The lower three are most connected to survival and our more animal instincts. Starting at the base of your spine is your Root chakra, the Muladhara, which is connected to your sense of being safe and secure. In your lower stomach you have your Sacral chakra, the Svadhisthana, which relates to your sense of creativity, sexuality, and emotions. Four fingers up from your Sacral is your Solar Plexus, the Manipura, connected to your sense of worth, your will, and your personal power in the world. Your Heart chakra, the Anahata is in the centre of your chest, and is your ability to receive and give love. The heart is the seat of the soul and connects you to compassion and your wholeness. Your Throat chakra, the Vishuddha, links to your ability to freely express your truth. Your third eye, the Ajna, in the centre of your brow, is connected to your insight and intuition – the all-seeing eye. The Crown chakra, or Sahaswara, located at the top of your head, is connected to your higher consciousness and pure awareness.

Increasing awareness

As you spend time in contemplative, still practices such as meditation, you enhance your awareness. This allows you to expand your states of consciousness and really be able to see and know yourself. The two glands in your brain associated with the third eye and the Crown chakra are the pineal and pituitary glands respectively. These glands play an important role in sending signals to our whole body, as well as in our psychic awareness. The pineal gland produces melatonin, which helps you relax and fall asleep. The pituitary gland is known as the master gland as it sends messages to other glands in the body. It is where these glands and the essence of these two chakras come together that extrasensory perception is opened and experienced. It is this centre that is directly connected with raising our consciousness.

Brainwaves and states of being

How you feel in yourself and the consciousness you experience are connected to your brain chemistry. We have five brainwave states and they have different frequencies and uses for us. Beta is your standard brainwave when you are going about your normal life, awake and alert. It is on a range of 12–38 Hz. In a Beta brainwave you are most connected to your conscious rational-thinking mind. In Alpha states, the brainwaves slow down to 8–12 Hz, and you are in a relaxed, calm, lucid state. This is perfect for intuition and creativity, and is a meditative state. You are no longer thinking, and are in an imaginative, open state. Theta brainwaves are 3–8 Hz and they are spaces of deep relaxation and very deep meditation, and are perfect for reprogramming the subconscious – you experience these when you are asleep and dreaming, or in certain energy healing and hypnosis practices. Delta brainwaves are the slowest, going up to 3 Hz, and are what you mostly experience when you are having deep, restorative sleep and not dreaming. You can reach this state in very deep meditation, where your body feels asleep but your consciousness is awake, such as during a mystical experience. There is also more recent research about high gamma brain states – very alert states between 38 to 42 Hz – taking you into a higher consciousness associated with peak performance and high levels of cognitive functioning. Your intuition and senses are awakened more fully. This is also a state you can reach through meditation. Once your brain gets entrained and used to certain types of brainwaves, it is much easier to access and maintain them.

Nourishing and restful sleep

Having restful sleep is so vital to every part of your body working optimally, connecting to its natural intelligence, and enabling your nervous system to rest and digest. This is also when so much emotional processing happens, as well as assimilation of information on multiple layers of consciousness. Experiencing both Theta and Delta brainwaves each night is beneficial.

Finding stillness

Seek moments of quiet each day, for example taking some time to yourself in the morning before your responsibilities begin, or in the evening before you go to bed to connect with yourself and listen to what you need and what is really going on for you. These are great times of day as you are in theta states as you are waking up or falling asleep, so it's the perfect time to program yourself for the day ahead, or for the processing you need at night. This is also a time where new ways forward, or new ideas, might appear. You can take moments of quiet at lunchtime, or a few breaths before and after you do anything significant. Your stillness opens up a beautiful space where your intuitive wisdom can find you.

For practices to help you embrace stillness see pages 114-127

FREE
YOURSELF

Living an intuitive life is living life on your own terms. Not the terms of your ego or a society that keeps you trapped in the status quo. You need to become a ninja at discerning where your needs and desires are coming from. Are they truly arising from a place of freedom where you are honouring your unique journey through this life?

Freedom lies in breaking out of the conventions that society and your conditioning put on you, and that in turn you put on yourself, so that you are free from limiting beliefs and structures – and are in connection with your own wild soul. That way, you are no longer doing anything based on the rule that you "should". You know that your path is yours, and it doesn't look or feel exactly like anyone else's.

" "

IF YOU KEEP TUNING INTO YOUR INTUITION YOU CAN FIND THE SUPPORT YOU NEED

Be a leader

Cultivating your own inner freedom takes you beyond comparison and outside influence to a state of being where you honour your uniqueness and what you have to bring to the world. This allows you to live a life that is innovative, inspiring, and visionary. We need more leaders in this world, not followers. You are a leader; you don't have to be a CEO, or a parent, or a leader in a traditional sense. In this new paradigm, leadership isn't about power over people, telling them what to do, or ruling by creating fear. Leadership is about leading yourself, owning your own state of being, and living from your own intuitive wisdom. When you are free, you lead and guide yourself – which in turn gives permission to others around you to do the same. You inspire other people, and you find yourself in the right place at the right time for you. A true leader is guided by soul, not by ego.

Your own personal catch 22

Your ego is often the most developed part of you. It does a good job at protecting you, but has a tendency to take itself too seriously. Your ego is the part of your personality that is your mask –

that you put on for the world. It's the labels that you have gathered through life and the image that you have of yourself. The ego is caught up in your story of who you are, what has happened to you, and what you have. It reminds you of what you have to do, and at the same time gives you all the reasons for not doing it, often blaming other people or circumstances, or beating yourself up. It has a tight, rigid, impenetrable feel to it.

Some egos can keep you feeling better than everyone else and make you dominant, controlling, and rude. Other egos can keep you small, unworthy, and unconfident – feeling sorry for yourself and a victim. Your ego likes to compare yourself to others, like that annoying auntie that tells you every Christmas that you haven't done as well as her children did! Your ego can look for ideas from other people, instead of trusting yourself. Your ego can be susceptible to the narratives of the cultures that you are part of and blindly follow them. It can keep you overthinking and going over the same thoughts in loops, it can trap you in negative emotions because of the story it's creating, and it needs validation and external approval. When you live from your ego, you can get very upset over

the things people do if they don't live up to your expectations. And then waste so much time in anger, resentment, fear, disappointment, self-doubt, and anxiety. However, your ego is an important aspect of you, not something to fix or transcend or get rid of, but a part of you to make friends with. When you understand what your ego is doing, and why, you don't give all your power to it.

For example, your ego can take the voice of an inner critic. So whereas your intuition might say, "Go on, call him!" your inner critic might say "He won't want to speak to you, it will be humiliating." And just like that you have put yourself back in a box and shut down the possibility that had opened for you. The best way to recognize if it's your ego criticizing is that it'll tell you what not to do but will give no truly helpful advice on what to do instead. Your ego loves things to be the same as they are now, as it sees change as scary and worries that you won't be able to handle it.

You find great freedom in your life when you learn the tone of the different inner voices and what they are there for. You can thank that part of you for wanting to protect you, and then with some authority and humour say, "It's cool – I've got this!" You will find some challenges along the way, but if you keep tuning into your intuition you can find the support you need.

You aren't born with your ego; it develops to protect you in the world that you are raised in. This is where your limiting perceptions, beliefs, and thoughts are created. Learning to loosen your ego's grip on you opens up so much in your life. In fact there is so much "power" to uncover in the parts of yourself that you have disowned because you didn't think they would be accepted by society or other people, or were good enough. This is the place Carl Jung called the Shadow, and when you dive in and free all the repressed parts of yourself you locked up down there, you become freer, more creative, more intuitive, and more successful – on your own terms.

It's important that you don't disown any parts of yourself even if they are difficult and tricky to manouevre with. You can imagine it like this: you let your ego come in the car with you – it may whine about not wanting to go where you are going like a tired child, but you don't give it the steering wheel, and that way all of you is able to move forwards.

Your wild soul

As well as your ego, you have a wild and beautiful soul. It's unique and vibrant and has something to bring to this world. The ancient Greeks called the soul the psyche, which has a logical component to it that is connected to the divine. In Sanskrit it is called the Atman, meaning inner self – this is where referring to the soul as the true Self comes from. In Hinduism and yoga philosophy you can't achieve liberation (moksha) without self-knowledge, which is to understand your soul as akin to God, to recognize the divine and perfect within. You can call it your true self, or your essence, or your spirit. Your soul has a purpose and a special energy to it. You can often see it when you look into a baby's eyes (or anyone's eyes); something eternal and transcendent. That's why it is said that your eyes are the gateway to the soul.

Another aspect of your soul is that whilst it can get buried under ego and trauma, it is always there. You are born with it, and you die with it. Some traditions believe that your soul is passed from lifetime to lifetime. There is the phrase "sold your soul" when you have done something that takes you far away from this quality in yourself, for example purposely hurting other humans or becoming drunk with a love of money and power. Your wild soul is so much more than what you do for a living, where you live, what you have, or the body you live in. It connects you to your true nature; the wildness and expansiveness that you are. When you develop a relationship with your soul, you have love and acceptance for who you are, you can see how the circumstances in your life have benefitted you, and you open up life to having much more meaning and possibility. Through your soul you have a sense of self-worth that is not dependent on anyone or anything, and from here your ideas, desires, and preferences arise. You may be inspired by other people but there is no competition or jealousy. When you listen to your soul, you are never wrong; you simply evolve and learn lessons along the way. You have power and a unique expression. From the perspective of the soul, each one of us is perfect and equally valuable.

Find freedom

You are free when you realize that you are both limitless and capable of absolutely anything, and also a small piece in a much bigger puzzle. You are awakening into your sovereignty, living in a way where you allow your intuition to guide you towards the great and wonderful experiences available to you, and where you remain humble and generous. This is the path of the leaders of tomorrow. And from here we can co-create a beautiful future.

For practices to help you find freedom see pages 128–141

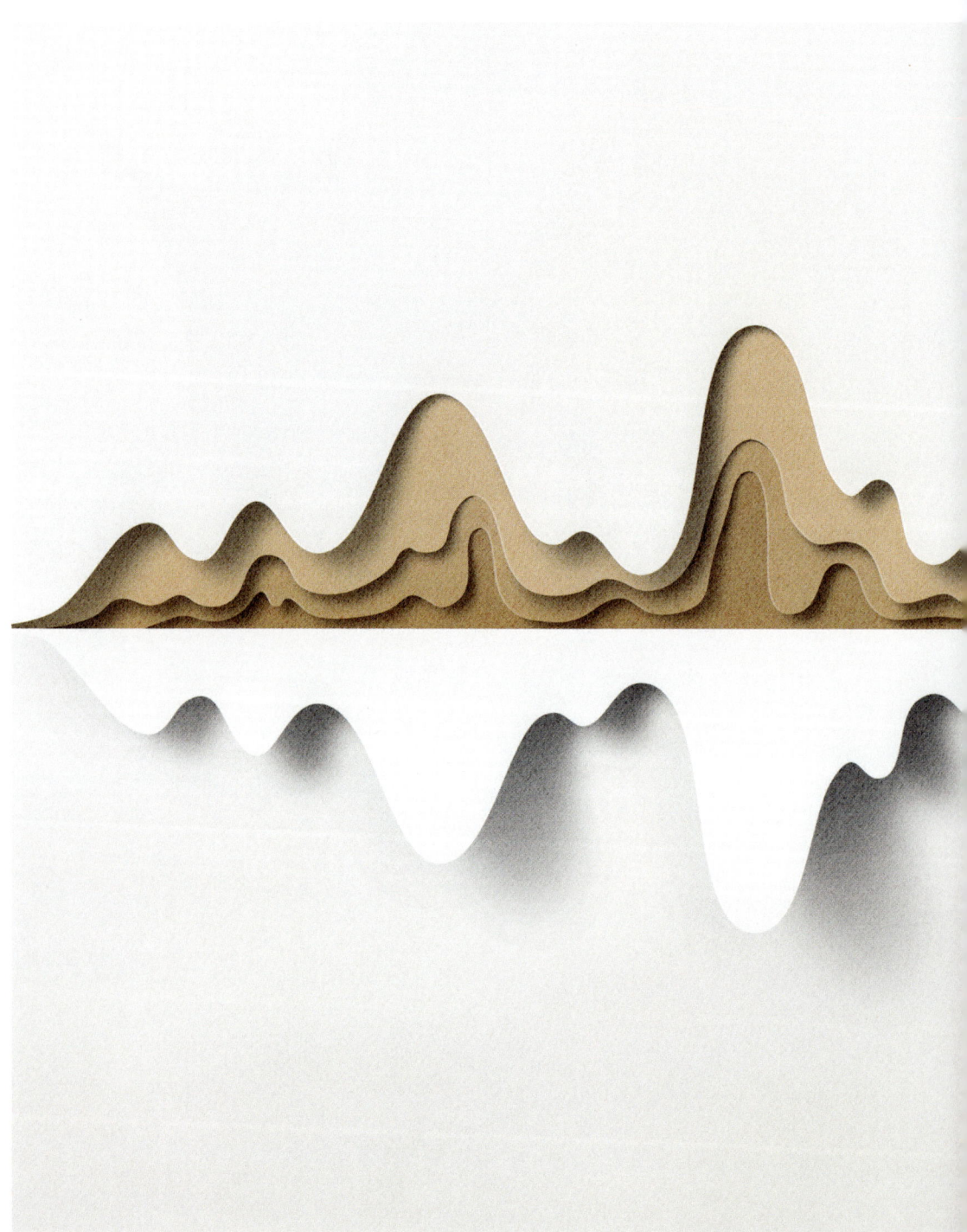

LISTEN

Learning to listen is key to receiving intuitive guidance, and to living in a way that keeps you open to learning new information and developing your intelligence. Listening will also increase both your awareness and understanding of the world – so you find the right place for you at the right time.

In most conversations between two people, no one is truly listening; commonly both people are listening only to work out what to say next. We have a need to be heard and are often seeking ways for this to happen. Most of what we hear or say is confirming our own bias of what we already believe to be true based on our worldview – which is based on the conditioning we have received over our lifetime and in particular during our childhood. The act of

" "

YOUR INTUITION IS LIKE THIS: A LOVING LOYAL FRIEND THAT WANTS TO SUPPORT YOU

listening to others opens up a deeper listening within yourself. It's an outside activity that assists with the inside path to your intuition; a modern artform.

Listening to your oldest friend

To truly listen means knowing how to embrace silence and hear what is being "said" in the pauses. From here you are able to pay attention to messages from your inner guide. For some people these messages come through an inner voice, but for others they are delivered through smells, synchronicities, or other people. For most of us it's a combination. In order to open to these listening channels fully, you need to move through any resistance you have to them. It's this resistance that is the most significant obstacle to your intuition. It can show up as you purposely ignoring or dismissing information as silly, or nonsense. Your resistance keeps you locked in your ego. Most of us had these listening skills naturally as a child before we were conditioned and told not to trust the voice – that it was strange or imagined. If you had a friend who was trying to tell you something, and called you up, but you put the phone down on them, texted you regularly but you never replied, popped over to your house but you didn't answer the door... then eventually that friend is going to get the message that you aren't interested in what they have to say. They will stop trying. Your intuition is like this: a loving loyal friend that wants to support you, and will keep finding ways for you to hear what it has to say, until it realizes that you are not interested. However, like the oldest of soul friends, all you have to do is pick up the phone to rekindle the friendship. Your intuition truly loves you and won't hold a grudge or punish you for ignoring it. It will simply begin to talk to you again.

Listening with all senses

We can listen not only with our ears, but with all our senses. Intuition is often called The Sixth Sense, a sense of knowing, as it relates to the sixth chakra. We commonly understand ourselves to have five senses; sight, hearing, touch, smell, and taste, yet we don't tend to use these senses to their full potential, or at least we don't talk about it if we do!

There are special names for senses that are developed into extrasensory perception, leading to what are called psychic gifts or abilities. They sound special, but they are available to all of us through a combination of natural preference and developing the skills. There is a spectrum for each of these. You have access to all of them. However, you may have one particular skill, or a combination of many, that is your natural style. Most of us have a dominant way of receiving and perceiving intuitive information, in the same way that we have a dominant style of relating, or a love language

Often your intuitive gifts will already be connected to what you do, or what you love in life or have a talent for. For example, a musician has clear hearing or a chef has clear tasting. You might decide what is right for you based on your senses without realizing. For example, what do you love about your favourite holiday spot? Is it the way it looks, or the way it smells, or the way it feels, or the soundscape, or the tastes? What stands out for you when you have an experience? What do you often tell others about?

The most powerful way to develop your own intuitive gifts is to work with what you have; find your uniqueness, rather than trying to mimic what somebody else has. It's the language of your soul, and when you find your unique style it opens up whole worlds and literal dimensions to you. Like anything, the more aware of it you become, if you are open and welcoming, the stronger your relationship with your intuition will be.

The Clairs

These different ways of receiving information are called the Clairs. There is information being broadcast constantly on different frequencies, like radio waves – you need to find out what radio channel you have reception for, and then tune in. Rather than understanding it as receiving messages from spirits, you can see it as an alchemical process that happens between you and the unseen world. Half of it is about how you translate the information you receive and set it in motion. Intuition loves action.

Claircognizance is clear knowing – the sixth sense. You might know things are going to happen before they do, or have knowledge of people you haven't met. You might seem to have a somewhat encyclopaedic knowledge of things you have never studied. This is the most advanced skill as it requires great trust to be able to communicate that you know when it's just a sense you have.

We all access this unconsciously in our survival intuition – for example you slow down your car just before somebody runs out into the road, or you decide not to get on the plane and then it crashes. This category could also include telepathy (being able to communicate without words); remote viewing (being able to see into a physical place or a person's inner world in real time); precognition (being able to see the future); retrocognition (being able to see the past); and other superhero-like skills.

Clairsentience and Clairempathy are clear feeling – you can sense how somebody else is feeling, be it emotionally or physically, or feel the energy in a room or in a story. You might get chills or a gut feeling that guides you towards knowing something – it is a recognizable signal in your body when something is true for you, such as pins and needles in your left foot. Sometimes it's an uncomfortable feeling; you know something is not right. Clairsentience is a clear physical feeling, whereas Clairempathy is a clear emotional feeling. This is common for people who are highly sensitive or empaths.

Clairvoyance is clear seeing, when you are able to see images flash through your third eye.

Some people need to close their eyes to be able to see – maybe visions in meditation – and others can see with their eyes open. The images can be strong, like a psychedelic trip, but are more often very light perceptual images. For some this also means they can see patterns of energy around people they meet – their auras – or they can see ghosts and spirits.

Clairaudience is clear hearing – the ability to hear words, music, or sounds through your inner voice. You might hear fully formed messages, or be able to "channel" or "download" whole books, songs, or speeches – the words just come directly to you in an effortless way.

Clairalience is clear smelling. This is when you are able to smell very strongly what is present, or use your sense of smell to lead you to something. Or you might even be able to smell something related to a memory, or to something that happened in a room – your deceased grandmother's perfume, say, or her cigarette smoke. Clairgustance is clear tasting – being able to taste something that isn't actually in your mouth. You might taste the favourite food of a deceased relative, or you may taste something that leads you to something for your future.

Clairtangency is clear touching. You can touch an object and know the history of it, or be able to receive knowledge about the previous owners. This is also called psychometry.

Experience deep listening

There is so much valuable information that you can tune into in the subtleties when you really pay attention. What can you notice in your own experience when you listen deeply? Allow your senses to be truly open and let your whole life come alive with all these beautiful messages.

For practices that will help you learn to truly listen see pages 142–153

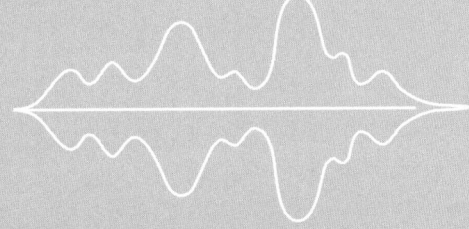

CONNECT

Connection is the heart of being. We are wired to connect – it brings meaning and beauty into life. When we are connected to ourselves, each other, and the earth our intuition can flow more freely and the collective consciousness of our planet can shift.

When you look at the way most modern societies are formed, it's easy to see that deep human connection has become less a part of the way of life. Many of us live alone or in nuclear families, we don't know our neighbours, we often connect with our friends through typed words and emoticons rather than by physical presence. We are constantly told we are individuals, that we can't trust others, or ourselves – we live in a cultural dynamic of separation. When in actuality we are part of a collective; we have shared hopes, desires, and feelings. This affects

" "

WHEN YOU SEE AND CAN LIVE CONNECTION OVER SEPARATION, YOU HAVE WOKEN UP TO THE TRUE BEAUTY OF THIS LIFE

us on an intuitive level as we are all impacted by the collective unconscious. Our intuitive insight allows us to see beyond the normal and literal walls between us and embrace the interconnectedness of life.

Intimately waking up

Intimacy can be broken down as "into me I see". The more you are willing to see yourself, be comfortable with yourself, and love yourself, the more intimate you can be with others and with the whole of nature and life itself. Being judgmental of yourself and others creates more separation, when we all need to be nurturing connection. Through the way in which you connect, your relationships, the way that you perceive the world, and the interplay of all things, you open yourself to live a life that is full of meaning, joy, and beauty. Knowing and respecting yourself is key to this. And understanding yourself as a part of a whole bigger experience takes the pressure off having to be everything, and instead means you can find your part in the greater story. When you see and can live connection over separation, you have woken up to the true beauty of this life and the true nature of existence.

The need for community

We don't live in this world alone. When you are comfortable with who you are, you are able to get closer to others and live more in connection and intimacy. The word community can be broken down into common unity – that which connects us. When we are able to relate to others from this place, it opens us up to deeper human connection. When we have communities that understand our journey and live from an intuitive place themselves, this opens up the field of possibility. Your intuitive insight becomes stronger around others who are also open, and vice versa, because the power of permission and the alchemical group field is strong. An integrated intuition becomes normal and this is so soothing for your soul.

Nature is alive

Indiginous cultures all over the world see nature as sacred and as forms of the divine, such as an understanding that we live with Mother Earth and Father Sky. Anyone who has taken a psychedelic drug or had a mystical experience – a moment where they merged into a feeling of total oneness – can tell you that everything is alive, open, and ready to talk to you. Nature isn't just land for us to build houses on or a place for us to grow food – it's a living, breathing organism of sophisticated intelligence and deep consciousness. Not only do the trees and plants provide resources and beauty, they are also receiving and transmitting consciousness. There are cultures that pray for the rain so the crops will grow, or dance for the sun. Those that understand rivers as goddesses, mountains as holy places. There are millions of people all over the world who travel on holy pilgrimages to receive the transmissions from sacred land. We are all part of this nature, connected to it, regardless of race, culture, or national identity. The earth has been here much longer than we have, and witnessed so many transformations. We can live in sacred reciprocity with the earth. All of nature is listening and ready to whisper intuitive wisdom to you as soon as you are ready to hear it.

Nature and the cycles of life

When you tune into nature's cycles of life, as we had to before we had 24/7 electricity and cities that never sleep, you can access deeper realms of intuitive wisdom. There are times of the day when the field of intuition is stronger, such as 4 o'clock in the morning just before everything starts to wake up and get busy. The cycles of the moon affect how we feel and how in tune with our intuition we are. The seasons offer us different insights and gifts. When you can harness these moments, you connect into deeper realms of intuition.

The interconnected web of life

Everything in this universe is interconnected. We are all connected through billions of invisible threads, through the electromagnetic field of consciousness – a web of information that binds us together. At the exact same moment, multiple people around the world can be having the exact same realization. Through the morphogenetic fields it has been shown that the same species of animal in different physical locations across the world can experience a spontaneous transfer of knowledge, behaviours, and abilities. Often we receive the same ideas or wisdom at similar times, as these ideas have their tipping point into the culture-scape. Likewise, when there is a traumatic event affecting multiple people and fear and anxiety in the collective field increases, we all feel it. We are having a shared experience here. The more of us who can connect to loving, peaceful, grateful, inspired feelings, the greater their presence is in the field, and this can affect our global future.

You are powerful

You are a transmitter of energy as well as a receiver so all that you cultivate in yourself, you are able to share with others consciously and unconsciously. Those who can read this information through their own intuitive senses will see it, others will be affected by it but not able to understand why. You are powerful. Developing this really beautiful understanding of who you are, and the depths and the levels of your magnificence, means that this is what you share with those around you – and transmit to all of those who know you across space and time.

Everyone is fighting some battle, learning, evolving, growing in themselves – and every single person you meet carries within them the same magnificence, beauty, and transcendent nature that you do. You can choose what you pay attention to and what you mirror to others. Humans, animals, plants, and nature have been shown to be affected not only by the behaviour in their environment, but also by intention. This is even true of water –studies have shown that the vibration and structure of the water is completely different if you say or even think beautiful thoughts around it compared to violent ones. The crystalline structure of the water made elegant geometrical shapes when given loving words, and became fragmented when negativity was projected onto it. Humans are 50 to 75 per cent water, which means the words and energy we are exposed to have a similar effect on us.

This sacred life

It's quite an amazing thing that you are here – that all your ancestors survived through so many stages of evolution, and that you were born into the world and are still alive. You are more than an economic being, here to grow the economy and do what you are told. You are unique and beautiful. You are a soul. Understanding your life as sacred doesn't mean you have to be religious or spiritual, it is simply that you are not taking your life for granted. Your consciousness can take you way below and way above the surface of a transactional reality, to really experience the

divine nature of being alive. Your rituals bring visibility to the invisible. Through connection you bring more lightness, more wonder, more joy, more creativity, and more collaboration into your world. Intuition loves this interplay between all things and these higher frequencies. The more that you can open up to experience this level of beauty, the more that exists in our collective consciousness.

For practices to encourage connection see pages 154–173

F L O W

Flow is your ability to live your life from a place beyond external control, where you are the architect of your own reality and live in the realm of unlimited possibilities – a place where flow states become flow consciousness.

Have you ever experienced moments of flow, where your default mode network turns off, and you find yourself living, creating, and truly loving life? You feel a sense of peace, and what you need effortlessly shows up. You feel blessed, generous, and open hearted. Life surprises you with its magnificence. You feel present, in touch with your divine wisdom. This is flow. It's the path of least resistance, where you can interact with the greater pattern of life in a way that is expansive. You might have entered a flow state when making art or music, in a moment connected to your purpose, or through a deep meditation.

" "

YOU HAVE THE POWER TO LIVE AN INTUITIVE LIFE, WHERE FLOW STATES BECOME FLOW CONSCIOUSNESS

Collective programming

As well as your personal subconscious patterning and belief systems – created by your upbringing, ancestry, and culture – there is programming within the collective conscious that impacts the beliefs that you have about life. Some common ones are that life is hard, you will be rewarded if you put the hours in, the faster you can go the more you will achieve. While it's true that you have to apply yourself to evolve, what is not true is that it has to be a struggle and a sacrifice. That is old paradigm thinking, and we are moving into a new paradigm for humanity as consciousness expands. There has been a tendency for humans to choose the hard route rather than the lighter more joyful path. The new way is a re-writing of "no pain, no gain" into letting the beauty of what you love guide you. As your personal consciousness expands it affects the collective consciousness and makes it easier for others to join you in the new paradigm.

Choosing inputs

We live in the age of information. Every day we encounter more language or data than humans ever have before. Advances in technology mean this has increased massively over the last twenty years with mobile phones and social networks. On top of this there is all the subconscious information that we pick up on. For example, you might not have noticed consciously what colour dress the woman who was sitting on a table opposite you at lunch yesterday was wearing, but still know when asked. We receive billions of pieces of information but only process a very small percentage of it. You have to choose your filtration system in order to decide what to pay attention to and manage. This selection will determine what is most prevalent in your bodymind, and shape your experience of life. The field of reality contains all of it, and you either consciously or unconsciously pick a lens through which to experience. Of course this gets more complicated to understand and nuanced if you live in a war zone or there is a natural disaster affecting your home. With a global pandemic, you can see it as a collective initiation, and still choose how you respond to it.

So much of your experience depends on how you frame it. For example, if you are obsessed with everyone being thinner than you are, that's what you will notice. If you have a belief that the world is a scary place, you will keep seeing opportunities for or experiences of danger. If you believe that people are kind and generous, you will be shown multiple examples of this generosity. If your new love interest has a soft spot for pineapples, you will start to notice pineapples everywhere. If there is a natural disaster affecting your community and you believe in rallying together, this is what you will experience. This faculty chooses what captures you based on what you have given the most attention. This is how you create your reality.

Synchronicity

When you place importance on your intuitive voice, you will experience what you might have previously called coincidences. You could have an intuitive idea, and then the next day somebody calls you up suggesting you work together on an idea they have had (not knowing it was similar to what you had already been wanting to do), and then you go for a coffee and bump into somebody in the queue who has the expertise or the contact you need, and so on. These are synchronicities that mean you are in flow and on the track that is perfect for you.

Presence and flow states

When you reach a state of flow, you are in an altered state of consciousness, a temporary experience of peak performance. You have full presence. There is no story running through your mind. There is no past and no future. You are creating, writing, singing, talking, reading, running, meditating, painting... whatever it is, with no awareness of time. Sometimes time feels like it slows down, or speeds up – you felt like it was five minutes when it was three hours, or you accomplished so much that the whole day passed in what felt like just an hour. You are completely in tune with your intuitive senses, and you are allowing yourself to be fully guided in an effortless and joyful manner, with full focus and clarity. There is no resistance.

Flow consciousness

You have the power to live an intuitive life, where flow states become flow consciousness. It's not a temporary moment you achieve, but a permanent way of being and relating with the world. This is similar to the Daoist concept of wu-wei, which means effortless action. There is a Sanskrit word that comes from the ancient Indian yoga tradition called pratibhā. It simultaneously means intuitive insight, embodied instinct, and creative inspiration. This inner wisdom leads you towards what is beneficial to all beings, as you weave together with the pattern of life itself. When you align fully and have broken free of your social and cultural conditioning, you have access to your pratibhā, and you create a life-experience of harmony. You may start out with glimpses or moments of it. Sometimes it's a quiet voice or something you can only see in retrospect. Other times it will be forceful and push you towards the things that align with your own nature or "essence". Pratibhā connects you to the greater flow of life – flow consciousness. The foundation of this is deep inner healing work, so that your conditioned patterns, past experiences, and limited beliefs don't keep adding resistance into the flow. You become very aware of how you frame your experiences. You free yourself to follow what feels the most light and expansive, knowing that you will evolve along the way but won't experience anything you don't have the consciousness to handle. Your intuition leads you into a life of your soul's wildest dreams, in harmony and balance with the greater intelligence of the universe. As you develop your intuitive skills, when you don't listen and don't follow through, you can really feel the consequences of this – a feeling that it's wrong, or even create dis-ease. You might have to go through some short-term discomfort to get to long-term satisfaction.

Constructing reality

When you live in flow consciousness, you understand that you are not a victim of what happens to you but that you have the power to create reality. Like the "edgewalkers" you can move between invisible worlds and translate information. Rather than be upset about an injustice that you see in the world, or feeling helpless, you are able to find your unique piece of the puzzle and bring something beautiful to the table. You can draw towards you and experience your visions of the future reality you want to create. Like yogis have for centuries, you can access the Akashic Records, which is like a hidden library in space where all knowledge of everything and everyone exists. You can enter the quantum field, which is a field of information beyond the material world – a realm of infinite limitless possibilities. The morphogenetic field, Akashic records, holographic universe, or quantum field are different names based on different traditions or scientific research that speak to the same thing – an intelligent infinite set of data available to you through intuitive clear knowing. Everything you need to know is available to you – you don't have to ask anyone outside of yourself, you don't need permission or validation or references from the past.

This is the natural state of being as we move into this new paradigm. Of course with great power comes great responsibility. You can choose to live an intuitive life of flow, and bring your soul's beautiful vision of reality here for all of us to experience and enjoy.

For practices that will help you to live life in flow see pages 174–181

TRUST

There are many things you can control, from what decisions you make and how you react, to what you choose as your reality, but you can't escape that in life many outcomes are unknown – this is where you draw on your trust.

We were made for these times. You have permission to trust in your life, your higher soul, and your intuition. Nobody can tell you if you are right or not. Only you know if it really was your intuition or your ego playing games. Creating this discernment to know your intuition is very personal. Through experience and bringing awareness to what works for you, you will understand and build trust. When embarking on a conscious path, we all need community and friends who are supportive to our growth and see the intuitive wisdom present in us. The vision we need to create a beautiful future is here in each of us.

Your inner voice

You need to really trust when your intuition is speaking to you – in whatever way it speaks. Your inner voice is unique and remember it is a part of you – it truly wants to guide you towards whatever is most expansive for you. Maybe hearing your inner voice feels warm, like being understood. Perhaps it's comforting or calming. It might be a feeling you get in your body, or a specific tone you hear, or the words that come out when you free write. It could be that you see obvious signs, like books fall off shelves in front of you on a page that holds the answer to your questions. Or your dreams may show you what you need to know.

Once you develop this relationship with your intuition you can take action. One of the most powerful feedback loops you have is to track what happened on past occasions where you followed your intuition and, on the other hand, times when you had a clear insight but did something different. Often, making an intuitive choice will not feel like the most logical thing to do according to society's standards, but there is still reason present. You may receive questioning or concern from those close to you as they can't see the reason behind your decisions, and you may not be able to explain it, or at least not in a way that gives satisfaction. Don't let others – or yourself – derail you from what you know is your own intuition.

Trust in who you are

We each have access to different resources and hold varying intersections of privilege and marginalization. There are systems of oppression at play that affect different people in different ways. For example, if you are black, brown, or indigenous – or female, trans, or disabled – you will often have to dig deeper into yourself and your wisdom to flow in a world that centres a white patriarchal world view. Remember that you are the wildest dreams of your ancestors, and don't just carry their trauma but the power of their survival and resilience. You have everything you need to be you. And you are changing the world as you live by your intuition and bring new paradigms into form.

Living in alignment with your soul

When you live from your intuition, you don't press a magic button where everything in your life will suddenly be amazing all the time. You are still a human being, living in this messy world, though your ability to navigate through will be stronger. You will live the life that is most in alignment with your soul, with who you are.

There are many different worldviews of what might be the meaning of life, but one universal understanding is that we learn, grow, and evolve. This is part of being human. Your intuition will guide you in the direction of your higher truth, what you need to learn, and the ways in which you need to evolve. Through your experiences and opportunities, you will learn exactly what you need for the next step. You will need trust as you navigate the uncertainty, along with the ups and downs. Can you trust through your challenges and be comfortable with the unknown?

The cycle of life

Life is a journey of transformation. It's cyclical, not a straight line where you go from beginner to expert. It's more holistic than that. You learn and you unlearn. You go through initiations. There is a basic cycle that you move through in life that starts with a wake-up moment, where you learn something you didn't know, you ask questions,

" "

YOU NEED TO REALLY TRUST WHEN YOUR INTUITION IS SPEAKING TO YOU – IN WHATEVER WAY IT SPEAKS

" "

YOU CONNECT TO A HAPPINESS OR SENSE OF PEACE IN YOURSELF THAT IS NOT DEPENDENT ON CIRCUMSTANCES

and find resources. This takes you into the grace period where you embody something new and feel that sense of achievement and satisfaction of having grown. Then from here you go into the honeymoon phase where everything flows and is wonderful – it feels like you have arrived where you always wanted to be. And then something knocks you off into the fall, which is always a surprise as you find that you no longer have everything together. You integrate what you have learnt and wake up again. You can go through this cycle multiple times a day, or be in one stage of this cycle for years. You may also find that you have overlapping cycles where you are at one stage with your romantic relationship for example, another stage with your career, and another with your health. We also have collective cycles that we are going through, which you can see easily through events like a global pandemic. Your intuition will tell you where you are in the cycle, when you can do something about it, what you can do, and when you need to just ride it out.

Evolving through trust

Often in life we meet the same kinds of challenges in different disguises. There is a powerful analogy of life being like a spiral staircase. You are climbing up this staircase, and you see the same wallpaper on the walls but simply from a different viewpoint. It's not the same yet it is familiar. Your challenges can feel like this – "I thought I had already resolved this one!" Ever had that kind of feeling? There is a fine line between getting stuck and repeating patterns unnecessarily, and evolving through the pattern so you understand it differently each time.

Trust allows you to hold where you have come from and where you are going, all in the present moment. It allows you to live with courage, resilience, and sovereignty. Trust means that you connect to a happiness or sense of peace in yourself that is not dependent on circumstances. You are able to trust in who you are, why you are here, and what you are learning. You find the simple pleasure of being you, whether it's a "good" day, "bad" day, or a really mediocre one. Your life isn't waiting for certain things to happen in order for you to be happy. You have cultivated a sense of joy, purpose, and trust in your life from your intuition – and that makes every day count.

From here life's mystery is an exciting place. You don't know what's going to happen but you trust in your role. Your intuition will guide you to do whatever supports your highest truth. This takes the fear out of life and worry out of what will happen, and instead opens you up to living life beautifully. As you do this with true humility and grace, you will be a sacred activist, stitching your threads into the weave of our beautiful future.

For practices that will help you to develop your trust see pages 182–187

THE
PRACTICES

HOW TO USE THESE PRACTICES

In our exploration of the principles of intuition you have been given a lot of information to digest. For some of you, something in there will have clicked and opened up your intuition, for others these practices will be the key that unlocks the door.

WHERE TO START

These practices support you in living from your intuition. Many of them will guide you to embody elements we have discussed in multiple principles, as your intuition is something present in you at all times through everything you do. Although you may find a practice within the Flow section, it can also support you in finding freedom, developing trust, creating space, or being open. Many of these practices work on several of the principles of intuition at the same time and provide ways to bring total bodymind awareness into your life. Some will be easy; others will be less comfortable. Some will take time to make a difference, while with other practices you may feel different instantly. Don't try to do all of them at once, or get stressed that you now have these on your to-do list.

Several of the practices will provide clarity when you need to make a decision and will help you open up to receiving clear direction from your inner voice, others will enable you to connect deeply with your true self. Some will bring you into bodymind alignment through movement or meditation, or take you into a flow state – essentially all part of the same coin. Bringing a selection of these practices into your daily life will ensure the door to your intuition is always open.

You can use your intuition to bring into your life the practices that you are drawn to at different times. Trust yourself to know what you need. There is one caveat to this, which is to notice the practices you are resistant to and give those a go. Sometimes you find the real gold when you move through your resistance. If you found one of the principles challenging, perhaps head to that section and begin there. You could start with the practice that excites you the most, or the one that seems the most odd to you. If you can't feel where to start, you could try closing your eyes and opening the book to a random practice and going with that.

CREATE NEW PATHWAYS

If something is unfamiliar to you and you haven't done anything like it before, then try it for 40 days in a row so that you can build new neural and embodied pathways, and really experience its benefits. It's called a "practice" as you are developing something over time.

These practices are designed to enhance your life and bring you more beauty, connection, and wisdom. It's a great blessing to be alive, and as you embody your intuition, let it be with a spirit of play and pleasure. Find presence in your life's great transitions, twists, and turns. Stay curious. And let yourself enjoy the process.

REST AND DIGEST

Taking time to rest and digest is so important to open up to an intuitive way of being. Rest is sacred and necessary. In a busy world, rest is a powerful act of resistance to the capitalist machine – a way of saying no and putting your inner self first. When you slow down, you make space to listen and to get to know yourself. In this space, new impulses can arise.

It can be easy to let the week pass with no good quality rest. Sleep deprivation, waking up to an alarm, scheduling activities for every hour of every day are all ways that we stop the natural flow of intuition. We so often keep life and the mind busy and full of things to do. You may fill your downtime with fun and social activities, rather than giving yourself space to fully rest, recharge, and develop your relationship with yourself. Seeing rest as a necessary part of your routine instead of a luxury is a total game-changer. It's making time for the part of yourself that isn't always productive, isn't always focused on things you have to do, or preoccupied with how people are viewing you.

Making space for rest can look as simple as having a few hours a week where you don't schedule social activities, family obligations, or work, and instead let yourself just be. It might also be that you take time to go away for a weekend or have a staycation

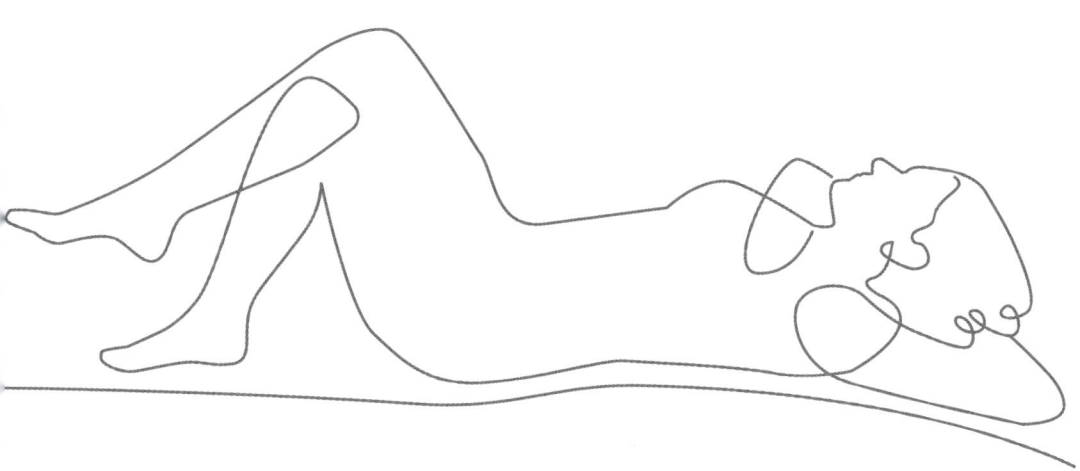

where you don't put any pressure on yourself to do anything. Let your intuition guide you towards what you need in order to refresh yourself in the short term, and this will give space for new intuitive wisdom about what might be important for you in the future.

Taking time out to go on a week's retreat, such as a yoga or silent meditation retreat, and having a proper break from your normal life pattern gives you a complete reset and opens up new pathways in your inner world.

BENEFITS Decolonize your life, replenish your system, rejuvenate.

TIME Make this a key part of your daily life.

DIGITAL DETOX

It's easy to become a slave to our technology, rather than using it as a tool that enhances life. When you are constantly responding to what is coming in through your phone it gets addictive and takes away from your space to connect with your intuition. In essence, taking a digital detox is about letting go of your attachment to your phone and everything that it opens up – feelings of comparison through social media, a sense of needing to perform for work, or checking to see if somebody has replied. In order to come out of the addictive pattern you can adopt these different detox strategies.

BENEFITS Clears headspace, new ideas and inspiration, deeper self-connection.

TIME The more the better – try 30 minutes each morning tech-free to start.

Notifications

Turn off all your notifications so that you don't get beeps or words flashing up on your screen constantly. That way you go into each app at a time that's good for you rather than every time you get a notification.

Night

Keep your phone out of your bedroom – maybe designate a basket where it gets placed by a certain time – so it's no longer the last thing you see at night and the first thing you see in the morning.

Detox Sundays

Give yourself tech-free Sundays where you don't even look at a phone or a computer. Even if you go out, you do it old-school and don't use your GPS or take any photos. Let your soul be your GPS and allow yourself to be fully in the moment.

Week off

To fully reset the habits that have arisen around your phone usage and dependence, give yourself a full week off every few months where you set up an out-of-office, turn off your phone, and enjoy what arises in the space.

When your physical space is full of clutter and mess, it can be another way of feeling so full that there isn't space for new information and seeing things from a different perspective. Taking time to clear clutter in your home and office can free up space for your intuitive voice, opening you up to new inspiration and clarity.

DECLUTTER

Desk

Clear your workspace by putting loose papers into boxes or trays. Place the things you need easy access to in a desk drawer. Only have what you need and a few things that inspire you in the space where you work.

BENEFITS Clarity, feel organized, open up to new perspectives.

TIME A little every day and a deep clear-out every New Moon.

Office

Make your office a haven of joy and clarity by clearing out any clutter and organizing the furniture so it feels calm, inspiring, and open. Make it a place where you want to be and where you feel in tune with your creative inspiration.

Online

Go through your email and social media accounts and unsubscribe or unfollow anything or anyone that doesn't either inspire you or provide you with useful information or tools for learning. Delete any apps that are mindless distractions.

Bedroom

Let your bedroom be a sanctuary of peace. Embrace minimalism and remove anything from the space that doesn't need to be there. Make it into a calm haven in your house that you associate only with rest and time for you or your relationship.

Wardrobe

Go through your wardrobe and give away clothing that you never wear to friends or charity shops. Keep only clothing and accessories that fit you well and that you feel good wearing. This will make getting dressed a simpler and more joyful process.

CREATE A SACRED SPACE

It's powerful to have a sacred space in your house that you come to as a place of connection to your intuition. It doesn't have to be a whole room; it can just be a corner or a small table that is your altar where you can celebrate your relationship to the higher aspects of yourself, whatever is most meaningful to you, and the earth.

BENEFITS Sacred connection, self-love, honouring, inviting.

TIME Tend to your sacred space every day and you will find that it will naturally expand.

1

Prepare

Find the place in your house that is perfect for your altar, where if possible there is plenty of space to sit in front of it. Place a table and either a cushion or a chair that makes you the perfect height to look comfortably at what is on the table.

2

Gather

Gather sacred objects that are precious to you – photos of family members, deities, or anything that you love. Arrange these objects around the edge of the table, leaving space in the middle for any intentions and prayers that are current for you.

3

Connect

Adorn your altar with plants or fresh wild flowers and some candles. Each morning when you wake up, come and sit at your altar for your meditation or simply to take a few minutes connecting to yourself and what is important to you.

CLEAR LIMITING BELIEFS

You have the power to clear your limiting beliefs that are holding you back from being fully open to letting your intuition guide you into a life of possibility.

1

Uncover

Go through the key areas of your life – relationships, career, health, home, contribution, and fun. For each area take some time to examine what you truly believe is possible, in terms of where the limits are for you. Write down each of these limiting beliefs.

4

Re-frame

Re-write your belief as something that is expansive and limitless, so you turn it around. As you say it out loud, rub your thymus (around the sternum) in a circular movement towards your heart. Repeat this re-written belief to yourself as often as possible.

BENEFITS Open to intuition, find freedom.

TIME Come to this every time you become aware of a limiting belief.

2

Disprove

For each belief write a list of all the proof you have that it is not true. For example, record experiences in your own life that have contradicted that belief and examples of others who have made it work despite similar potentially limiting circumstances.

3

Clear

Take one of the beliefs and repeat out loud that you are deleting or learning this belief. To assist the clearing, place the fingers from your dominant hand gently into your sternum as you do this. Clear one belief at a time.

5

Become aware

When you are triggered – something happens or somebody says something that sends you back into your limiting belief – you lose sight of what is possible. Learn what triggers you so that you can breathe into the emotion and let it pass rather than buying into the limiting story.

6

Trust

It can be tempting to feel like you can just erase the beliefs all at once, and whilst knowledge and awareness is a good start, each belief will need care and time. In order to change it, you need to believe this is just a story, and not the true you.

ADVENTURE

In order to keep yourself open to intuition, you need to break out of your usual habits and routines. An adventure is the perfect way to open up new pathways and welcome in a fresh perspective.

Your adventure might be going on the trip of a lifetime, taking up an extreme outdoor sport, or it could be as simple as going somewhere you have never been before, taking a different route on your way home, or saying yes to something that you would normally say no to. Adventure brings the spice and aliveness that welcomes an intuitive spirit. Sometimes getting a little lost can help you find your way.

BENEFITS Get out of your comfort zone, refreshment, energizing, new perspectives.

TIME Challenge yourself to be adventurous every day.

ENERGY HEALING

Understanding yourself as an energetic being is key to living in a deeper relationship with your intuition, and being open to heal yourself. When you begin to experience different aspects of your energy bodies, you understand much deeper aspects of reality. There are many worlds in the spaces between stories and labels, where so much of our experience lives. The more that you become aware of, and attuned to the energy in your own body, the more you will open to experiencing it everywhere. You learn to read energy, which is the form in which so much of intuitive wisdom communicates.

BENEFITS
Activates you as your own healer; attunes you to reading energy.

TIME Try to spend five minutes a day doing this.

1

Centre yourself

Sit down in a meditative posture and close your eyes. Connect to your breath, bringing calmness into your being. Feel the energy of the earth beneath you, and the energy of the cosmos above you. This practice will allow you to clear energy without words and activates your healing.

2

Prepare

Invite all energy that is not yours or is out of harmony to drain into the earth where it can be composted. Then state that you are calling your energy back into your body – so that any energy you have knowingly or unknowingly given away can be brought back to you.

3

Activate energy

Rub the palms of your hands together fast for about a minute, generating heat in your hands. Smile as you do this, connecting to your power. Pull your hands about six inches apart, palms facing each other. Feel the energy between your palms and in your hands.

4

Direct energy

Send this energy to anywhere in your bodymind that wants healing. You might place your hands onto your body, wherever they intuitively want to go. You can move around different parts of your body. When you feel finished, bring your hands into prayer and give thanks.

Having intentions is an incredibly powerful way to navigate life and invite in the unseen world. By setting an intention you are stating your part in the reciprocity of something new coming into being. Your intuition will guide you to what intentions to set as well as nudge you along to take steps towards making them a reality.

SET INTENTIONS

An intention is different to a goal as it is open and invites in the unexpected, so you might actually create something better than your wildest dreams. Your intentions can be both personal and collective. They become a guiding force, holding your values and supporting you to live in alignment.

Ways to set an intention:

- Have it reflect how you want to feel, for example "I feel curious and open to new experiences."
- Make it present, not an achievement in the future, for example "I listen to my intuition."
- Make it simple and expansive, for example "I love myself fully and am open to new healthy relationships."
- Have it reflect your values, for example "I value living sustainably."

It's a good idea to write out your intentions and place this piece of paper somewhere you'll see it when you wake up, or on your altar so you connect to it each morning. You can also get into the habit of connecting to your intentions by saying them to yourself at regular points in the day, for example at the start of yoga, before a meeting, on your way to a date, and so on.

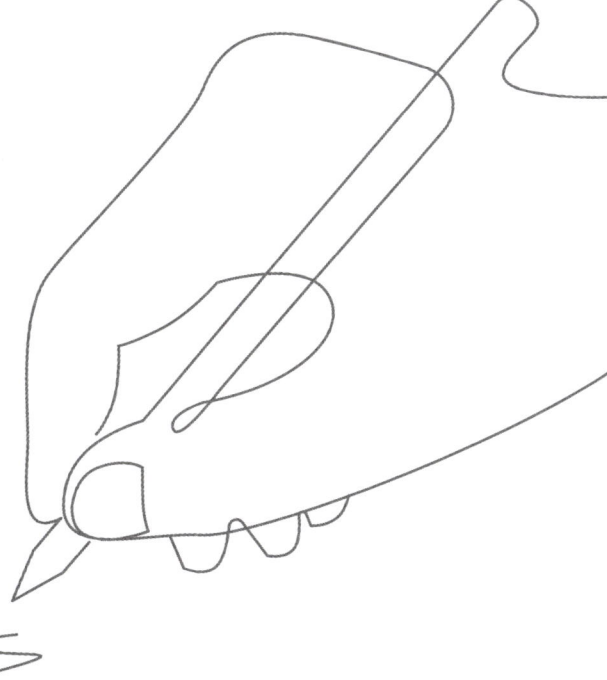

BENEFITS
Opens a pathway
to your higher self.

TIME Make daily
intentions, and deeper
soul intentions whenever
you need to invite
change into your life.

MINDFUL MOVEMENT

Movement is the key to embodiment. To feel the alignment in every cell of your bodymind – and through the centres in your head, heart, and gut – you need to move your body.

This coherence creates a container that the wisdom of your own intuition can reside in. The movement can be anything that feels good in your body, and that perhaps you already do, that offers solo time and repetition such as walking, running, cycling, or swimming. The nuance here is that you set an intention to open up your bodymind to receive your intuition as you engage in the activity. You could even state a question that you want to hear the answer to.

BENEFITS Enhanced physical health, physical connectedness.

TIME Minimum of 20 minutes a day.

Yoga is a sophisticated ancient technology for turning on the bodymind to be a full receptive vessel for lived intuitive insight. The word yoga means union or to yoke, and the practice is a cultivation of a subtle internal state. It's a path of self-mastery that gives you the skills to respond to life rather than react.

YOGA

Through practising yoga, you experience yourself in your own true nature, which is divine. There are many aspects of yoga practice, including asana (the physical postures), mantra (chanting sacred sounds), mudra (sacred hand gestures), pranayama (breathwork), dhyana (meditation), sadhana (spiritual practice), darshana (philosophical view), and upaya (skilful methodology). There are also principles that guide your practice: having a sankalpa (intention), and the tattvas (principles) of iccha (creative impulse), jnana (insight), and kriya (action).

Through cultivating a yoga practice, you are expanding your experience of your bodymind and how you relate to reality. The physical practice brings both strength and flexibility. It teaches you how to centre yourself and bring aliveness and coherence into your whole bodymind. Through yoga you can release trauma and stuck emotions that can blur your intuition. Yoga teaches you

to live in a state of ananda, which means unconditional bliss. This is a bliss that is not dependent on what is happening in your life, but means you love the whole spectrum of aliveness, where you can embrace your joy as well as your suffering. A dedicated yoga practice is truly life changing.

Yoga is an incredibly powerful practice for both connecting you to your intuition and supporting you in living in a way that is embodied, natural, and graceful.

BENEFITS Self-mastery, embodying true potential.

TIME Yoga is a way of life that with practice becomes a way of being.

When it comes to your yoga asana practice, the deeper and more regular your practice is, the more beneficial it will be for the cultivation of your intuition. It's important to find a teacher who you resonate with, who can take you through experiences and give you guidance that is attuned to your bodymind and where you are at physically, emotionally, and spiritually. This is a simple starting sequence that you can begin with at home that will bring your bodymind into alignment. Move with your breath.

YOGA ASANA

BENEFITS Embodiment, attuning, release.

TIME This sequence will take around 15 minutes, depending on how long you stay in each pose.

1

Easy pose

(Sankalpa Mudra in Sukhasana)

- Sit down cross-legged with your spine straight and close your eyes.
  You can sit on a folded blanket so that your hips are higher than your knees. Chant the sound Om.
- Place your right hand on your right knee, palm open facing upward. Place your left hand on top, clasping the hands.
- Bring into your awareness your intention for this practice. It could be to strengthen your relationship with your intuition.

2

Mountain pose

(Tadasana)

- Stand up with both feet planted firmly on the ground, inner hip distance apart.
- Hug your shins towards each other so you activate the muscle energy of your legs. Push your thighs back.
- Lift up through your rib cage, draw your shoulders back, lift your chin.
- Take three deep breaths, feeling this clear alignment in your bodymind.

3

Crescent lunge

(Alanasana)

- From mountain pose step your left foot back and lift your left heel so only your toes are on the earth – you can either lower your left knee to the ground or keep it lifted depending on your body or energy levels.

- Check that your right knee is positioned directly above your right ankle. Lift up through your left thigh if it is lifted. Raise your arms up to the sky and stay here for ten breaths.

- Swap sides so your right foot is back and your left foot is forward, positioned directly above your left ankle.

4

Humble warrior

(Baddha Virabhadrasana)

- Step your left foot back and place it on the ground in Warrior I pose, meaning you place your left foot fully on the ground, turned out towards the left.

- Interlace your hands behind your back. Take a deep inhale, and then on the exhale pour your heart forward with humility, bringing your right shoulder inside your right knee.

- Relax your head, neck, and shoulders. Take five deep breaths here before gently lifting your head.

- Step your left foot forward, and repeat with your right foot back.

5

Pigeon pose

(Eka Pada Rajakapotasana)

- From mountain pose, place both hands on the ground so you are in a standing forward bend. Step your feet back to downward facing dog.

- Lift your left foot up to the sky on an inhale, and on your exhale place your left knee to the ground outside of your left hand. Release your right knee to the earth, toes to the ground and square your hips to the front of your mat.

- Interlace your fingers and bring your elbows and hands to the earth in front of you. Breathe here for 15 breaths.

- To come out, place your hands under your shoulders and rise back into downward facing dog. Take the second side.

6

Full body staff

(Danda Pranam)

- Lie down straight on the earth, stomach and head facing down.

- Place your arms straight out in front of you with your hands joined together in anjali mudra (prayer position). Make an offering of your intention with your whole body (the word Pranam means offerings).

- As you breathe, feel a sensation of surrender and release. Stay here for 15 breaths, or longer if your intuition guides you to.

- As you make your way out, use your hands to push yourself back to a kneeling position.

DANCE

There is nothing like free-flow dance to both release stuck emotions from the bodymind and open up to new creativity and insight. It's the kind of dancing that you do in your bedroom when nobody is around where you put on your favourite upbeat or weepy songs and let your body move however it wants.

BENEFITS More liberated sense of being, enhances rhythm, receive insights.

TIME Let yourself go and become absorbed into the music for a full hour or two.

Letting your intuition guide your movement opens you up to allowing your intuition to guide every aspect of your life.

When you are ready to leave the safety of your bedroom there are places where you can go and dance with others, in this intention of free flow movement. You can try Five Rhythms dancing, which is a beautiful silent space of dance where you move through a wave of five different tempos of music, from flowing to staccato to chaos to lyrical to stillness. If you want something that is less of a process but still a silent soulful experience, you can try ecstatic dance. And for a fun sober dance with your friends where you can chat just like those nights in the clubs, try out the early morning raves.

Dancing is a moving prayer that opens up an aliveness in every cell of your being, where you can feel closest to yourself, to life, and to a higher consciousness.

EMBRACE EMOTION

*Emotions are a natural part of life, energy in motion,
but when they get stuck, they fog up your intuition.
It can be common to only show positive emotions
and in some cultures not too much – even joy can be
frowned upon. Something very powerful happens when
you embrace your emotions. They don't need a story;
they just need to move through you. You can embrace
both so-called positive and negative emotions.*

1

Name it

When you experience a strong
emotion resist any urge to repress it.
Name the emotion – such as "I am
feeling anger" – but don't create a
story about why you have it.

BENEFITS
Enhanced life
experience, clarity,
release.

TIME Give yourself
five minutes for
powerful emotions.

2

Feel it

Feel where the emotion is alive
in your body and, if it's helpful, give
it a colour and a shape. Breathe into
the emotion without trying to make
it go away.

3

Release it

If you can, release your emotion
then let it flow away from your body
– but don't direct the emotion at
anyone. Remember this too
will pass.

GUT CHECKER

In order to get a feel of what your bodymind wants without having to think about it, a lovely technique is the gut checker, where you turn your whole body into a pendulum through which to receive your intuition. Come to this when you're looking to make a decision or for clarity on a situation.

BENEFITS
Bypass the mind to get intuitive insights.

TIME It takes less than one minute for an answer to come.

1

Centre yourself

Stand up nice and tall with both feet on the ground, inner hip distance apart – note this doesn't work well in high heels. Close your eyes and relax your breath for around 20 seconds to centre your self.

2

A yes response

Say "Show me yes" – for most people you will find that your body tips forward as you are drawn towards something. The movement might be very subtle or you may feel like you are almost falling over.

3

A no response

Say "Show me no" – for most people you will find that your body tips backwards away from something. Start with some test questions that have an easy yes or no answer, such as "Is my name...?", or "Do I live in...?" and test your body's response.

4

Ask questions

Ask a question with no "shoulds", like "Is it in my best interests to take this job?" Or you might hold a bottle of vitamins and ask "Does my body want this for healing?" See which way your body tips and this is your answer.

Through nutrition you impact the functionality of your whole bodymind. Your gut is so interlinked with how you feel and think, as well as the layers of consciousness you are able to embody. We are all wired slightly differently, so you have to experiment in order to find which foods and supplements work best for you.

NUTRITION

Sometimes you may want to eat heavier in order to desensitize and ground yourself – bringing your energy down into your stomach and your root. At other times you might want to consume lighter foods in order to bring your energy into the higher parts of your body, such as your brain and heart.

As your microbiome is so key to your overall experience of life, it pays to be kind to it. Some things that you can let go of in general are processed foods, so you eat only fresh and vibrant meals. A plant-based diet can be really elevating, cutting out meat and dairy which are heavier in their nature and weighed down with more history in terms of how the animals were treated. Processed sugars are best avoided as they affect both your health and access to your intuition. Eating in a way that is healthy, organic, and home-cooked will also reduce toxins and inflammation.

It's important to ensure that you are always well-hydrated, drinking water that has been filtered or is from a spring. Try to eat plenty of leafy greens and high protein foods such as lentils, chia seeds, broccoli, almonds, and avocados, as well as choosing foods that are local and in season, and foraging for wild superfoods. The mitochondria – the parts of your cells that generate energy –

love the polyphenols from herbs, spices, coffee, tea, and chocolate. Including these in your diet can improve brain function as well as your gut health.

Practices like mono diets, cleanses, and intermittent fasting can help to detox your system by giving your bodymind more time in rest and digest mode. Adding foods such as cacao, apple cider vinegar, and tamarind to decalcify your pineal gland – which corresponds to the third eye, your centre of intuition – can be helpful.

The healthier your bodymind is, the more energy you will have to both deal with your day-to-day life and explore unseen realms.

BENEFITS
Longevity and a greater quality of life.

TIME Pay attention to everything you put into your body temple all of the time.

Biohacking is when you enhance your experience of your bodymind by consciously changing your chemistry and physiology. We have access to amazing technologies, supplements, and innovations that can support you in not only living a healthy life, but can optimize your performance and your human potential.

BIOHACKING

There is always new research and many innovative products coming out that can change your experience of living in your bodymind. One such tool – a small wearable device that gives you biofeedback – has the ability to measure your heart rate variability. This lets you know when you trigger your autonomic stress response, so that you can then work to bring yourself back into a state of coherence.

As we have more devices in our life, we also need to learn how to mitigate the negative impacts of EMFs (electromagnetic frequencies) so your field can be in harmony.

There are many supplements that can support your intuition, from high-quality multivitamins through to nootropics that boost brainpower, and certain strains of probiotics that can assist with your gut health. Be open to trying new things and expanding what you engage with, as we are constantly redefining what being human means and what is available to us through science and technology.

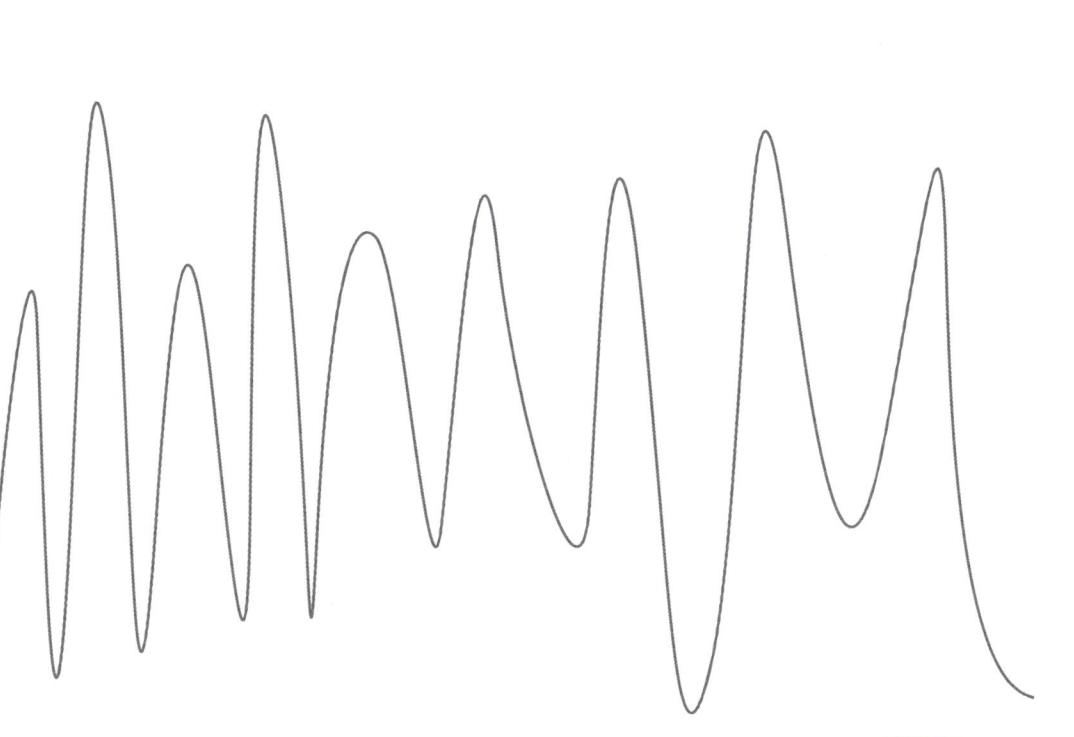

BENEFITS Enhanced senses, increased health, inner attunement.

TIME Research regularly and try different things to see what works for you (not everything at once).

SILENCE

Spending time in silence creates the stillness in which your intuition can talk to you. It's very normal in society to fill all spaces with conversation or noise. Learning to be comfortable in the silence is a powerful skill; so much beauty happens in these pauses.

Think of that phrase "silence is golden". In order to bring more silence into your life, you can experiment with giving yourself blocks of time when you have no distractions such as phones, or people you are in direct conversation with. It could be as simple as sitting outside during your lunch break in silence. Or you might choose to have a silent day once a month or once a week, and get everyone in your household to either join in or not talk to you. Or you could have silent mornings, where nobody talks for the first few hours of the day and see how this changes the quality of your conversation as well as the insights you receive. You can go on silent retreats if you want a whole week's experience, or even create your own sanctuary of silence at home.

BENEFITS Refining the inner voice, deeper sense of peace.

TIME Start with small periods of silence, and work your way up to as many pauses as possible.

MEDITATION

Meditation is the most key practice when it comes to developing a relationship with your inner world and therefore your intuition. Knowing how to sit with yourself opens up these gateways to being able to hear the wise intuitive voice, as well as getting to know the different voices in your head so you can discern between intuition, stories, and fear. Take a sacred pause to re-centre.

1

Space

Find a quiet space where you can sit and meditate. If at home, this may be in front of your altar. You might want to start somewhere quiet, but as you practise more, you will find you can create a meditative space anywhere.

4

Mudra

Place your hands on your knees with your palms facing up if you feel more open to receive and give, or with your palms facing down resting on your knees if you want to focus more on grounding and your own internal energy.

BENEFITS Know yourself, focus, silence, peace, improve overall health and wellbeing.

TIME This practice can be done for anything from two minutes to an hour, with 20 minutes being a sweet spot.

2

Posture

Sit up nice and tall, ideally on a cushion if you are on the floor so your hips are higher than your knees and you can sit comfortably for a while. If on a chair, make sure your feet are placed firmly on the ground.

3

Intention

Close your eyes and tune into your intention for your meditation practice. This could be simply to stay present in this moment, or to develop a deeper relationship with your intuition.

5

Breath

With your eyes still closed, consciously slow down your breath for ten breaths. Make your inhale long and slow; fill your belly and chest with air, and then exhale slowly and completely. After this let your breath find its own slow rhythm.

6

Focal point

Choose a focal point of either your heart or your third eye. Breathe into this place, and feel yourself looking out through this centre. As your thoughts come up, just notice they are there, label them as thinking and bring yourself back to your breath.

If you live in an over-stimulated state most of the time, it's impossible to give your subconscious the stillness that it needs to process inputs, and your bodymind enough time in rest and digest. Taking short daily practices of yoga nidra can provide you with high quality rest whenever you need it.

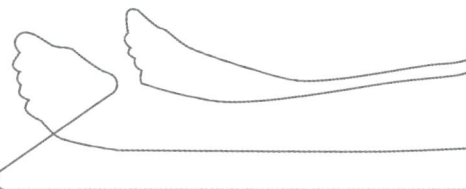

YOGA NIDRA

Yoga nidra is a practice of yogic sleep where you lie down and are guided into a state of effortless relaxation through the teacher's voice. During yoga nidra you can experience different brainwave states and have the most restful nap, whilst also allowing processing in your subconscious, which is really beneficial for your intuition. With yoga nidra you welcome yourself home, and connect to the truth of who you are. Though it feels like you are doing nothing, you will feel its replenishing and rejuvenating effects.

As you feel your body in this practice, through the guidance, you enter into a rest and digest state. Your brainwaves go from beta to alpha to theta and then into delta. Your thoughts slow down, you process emotion, and your organs regenerate and metabolize cortisol – moving this stress

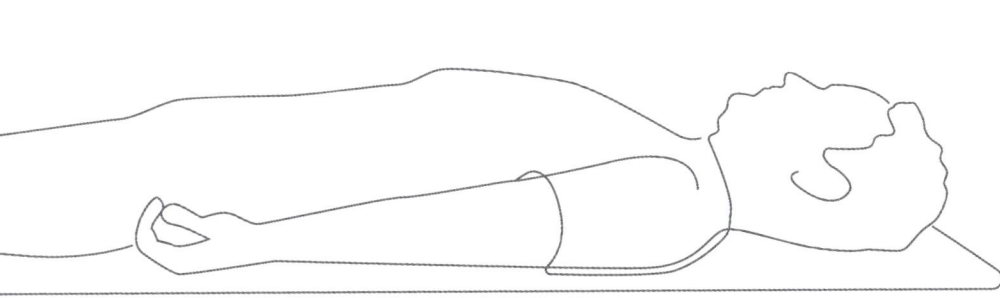

hormone out of your body. In this space you are creating a more committed relationship with your inner world as well as giving your bodymind what it needs. To practise yoga nidra, you need to be guided by a skilled teacher. This can be through an audio that you listen to – there are many apps and guided yoga nidra meditations online – or by going to a specific yoga nidra class or retreat with a live teacher.

BENEFITS Deep rest and healing, processing of subconscious. **TIME** Whenever you feel you need a rest. Can be great for a true "power nap" or to help you sleep at night.

SOUND HEALING

Music has codes within it that affect how you feel, what you think, and the quality of your intuition. Sound healing transports you into a place of stillness where you can access the voice within.

Bring music into your life in a way that is healing, expansive, and takes you into unseen parts of yourself. Something magnificent happens when you lie back, close your eyes, and let yourself be absorbed into sound. It could be soulful jazz, bhajans, or classical piano. Sound has an elegance, with the energy of who created it and their intentions woven through. Choose music that you find relaxing, spiritual, and uplifting. You can use binaural beats to take you directly into alpha, theta, or delta brainwaves so you can access a deeper aspect of your intuition.

Sound healing is also a powerful group experience, which can be felt through live healing events such as kirtan, sacred singing, sound bowls, or gong baths where you can turn off your rational mind and rest in deep theta and delta states – to refresh, restore, heal, and come into clarity.

BENEFITS Activates deeper states of mind.
TIME Bring high vibration into your life as often as possible.

PRANAYAMA

Pranayama is the name for breathwork in yoga. Prana means lifeforce in Sanskrit, yama means to retain, and ayama means to extend – so it's the extension and retainment of lifeforce. This is one of the key practices that can bring you into a state of stillness and coherence. Through this practice you are opening the channels of your intuitive wisdom. Choose from these three techniques the breath that will support you in this moment.

Sama Vritti

(Equal breathing)

- To begin, sit up nice and tall in a meditative position – this can be on the floor or on a chair.
- Sama Vritti is a simple breath where you breathe consciously in equal parts.
- Place your hands on your knees. Inhale for a count of five, hold in for five counts, exhale for five counts, hold out for five counts. Repeat as long as desired. You can change the breath count to suit you.

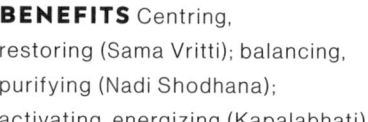

BENEFITS Centring, restoring (Sama Vritti); balancing, purifying (Nadi Shodhana); activating, energizing (Kapalabhati).

TIME A few minutes or much longer, whenever you need them. If you are pregnant or on the first days of your moon cycle, please don't do breath retention or Kapalabhati. During this time focus on slower, deeper breaths.

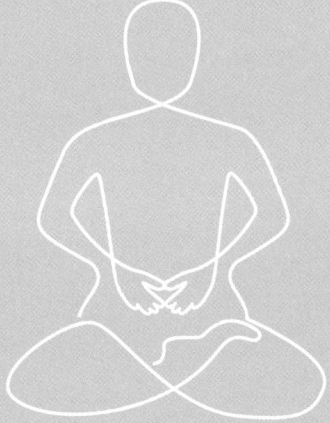

Nadi Shodhana

(Alternate nostril breathing)

- Close your eyes, place your left hand on your left knee, palm up.

- Place your right index and middle fingers onto your third eye. Place the tip of your ring finger over your left nostril and your thumb on your right nostril.

- Cover your right nostril and inhale through the left. Cover your left nostril and exhale through the right. Inhale through the right, exhale through the left. Continue for three minutes.

Kapalabhati

(Breath of fire)

- Rest your hands on your belly and take a few deep breaths.

- Start to release short, strong, and active exhalations through your nose. Pause at the end of each exhalation. Focus on the exhalations and let the inhalations be passive.

- Feel a pump in your belly on each exhalation, as your belly draws in. Do this for one minute and then let your breathing gently return to its normal pattern.

CENTRES OF POWER MEDITATION

You have three main centres of power. As you form a stronger relationship with your subtle body and an awareness of energy, you can find stillness in a moment and decide where to centre yourself. You can create coherence in your bodymind and embody the wisdom of your intuition.

BENEFITS Centring, embody empowerment.

TIME 20 minutes.

1

Prepare

Sit in a meditation seat or stand up nice and tall with your feet inner hip distance apart. Close your eyes. Notice your feminine energy on the left side of your body and the masculine energy on the right side, and draw them both into the central channel.

4

Heart chakra

Bring your awareness up into your heart space, and breathe here. Feel connected to your openness to give, receive, and be love. Feel a ball of light the colour of green grass. Feel this green light of your heart energy move out, creating a circle around you on the horizontal plane. Soften into this space for five minutes.

2

Lower chakras

Start by feeling a connection to the ground and becoming aware of your root, sacral, and solar plexus chakras. Connect to a sense of being rooted, grounded, safe, creative and empowered. Bring your awareness and your breath into your belly.

3

Visualize

As you breathe into this centre point imagine a ball of light in your belly, the colour of fire, and feel the energy from here come out in every direction. Imagine it travelling horizontally through your whole energy field. Stay in this centre for at least five minutes.

5

Upper chakras

Now move your awareness up into your head centre. Feel your throat, third eye, and crown chakras as you open to your divine connection and your knowing. Bring your attention to rest in the centre of your head. Expand your energy out to make a circle on the horizontal plane. Stay in this centre for at least five minutes.

6

Re-centre

Now notice how different each centre feels, and choose the centre that you want to rest your power in. Bring your awareness and your breath to this centre. Open your eyes and keep your breath here. As you become more skilled in this, you can skip to this step any time you need to re-centre.

BATHING

There is something about submerging in water that can bring insights, wisdom, and clarity. The benefits of bathing can be enjoyed in nature or from the comfort of your own home.

BENEFITS More liberated sense of being, enhances rhythm, brings insight.

TIME Let yourself go and become absorbed into the music for a full hour or two.

You could bathe in an outside body of cold, revitalizing water such as a natural spring, a lake, or a waterfall. Or it could be a cosy bathtub with Epsom salts, candles, flower petals, relaxing music, and your favourite essential oil. Set an intention, or have a question in mind that you want some clarity on before you bathe, and then let go. Make it a ritual and give thanks to the water. You can even do this in your daily shower.

Salt water cleanses your energy – you can rub your body with salt in the shower, get in the sea, or even put your feet in salt water while you are sitting down.

NAME INNER VOICES

One of the biggest questions many have is how do I know if it's my ego or my soul talking to me? How do I know if it's really my intuition? Which part of my inner guidance can I trust? We all have voices in our head – learning to differentiate between these is key as it allows us to free ourselves from our limiting voices and choose wisdom.

BENEFITS Clarity, self-love, comedy.

TIME Make this a daily practice, observing your inner voices throughout the day.

1

Recognize

Notice the different types of limiting voices that you have in your head. You will find that you have many. The "ego" voices were picked up along the way to protect us from harm. Start to recognize all the voices as different characters.

4

Tame the voice

These characters make themselves heard in order to keep you safe the best way they learnt how when you were a child. So with this in mind you can treat them much as you would a child who doesn't have all the information – with guidance and love.

2

Ego voices

To identify the ego voices, notice how they have a way of showing you a problem without offering a solution, plus they like what's familiar. When the default mode thinking network is activated in the mind we find ourselves in endless self-absorbed monologues with these voices.

3

Name the voice

Give each character in your head a name such as Nagging Nina, Scared Shipla, Pessimistic Paul, or Judgmental Jamal. Let them become more like caricatures. By categorizing them in this way their influence and hold over you becomes diminished.

5

Soul voices

Now name the wiser voices of your soul. Maybe this is one clear distinct voice, or could be a series of characters. These voices are encouraging and wise. They believe in you, they know why you are here. This is the inner voice that will free you from the ego.

6

Distinguish

When your inner dialogue begins this does not mean you are crazy – we all have many voices in our head. You can now either listen fully to the wise voices, or turn to the limiting ones with curiosity and kindness – not needing to either do what they say or reject them.

TAME THE INNER CRITIC

The inner critic is dangerous to your intuition as this is the voice that stops you from listening to your guidance and being free. For many it is so loud that it drowns out the inner nurturer who brings encouragement and self-compassion. If your inner critic is super inflated, you need to tame it!

1

Listen

Next time you notice that your inner critic is in overdrive – stop and listen. Invite it to go full throttle and tell you what it really thinks. Take a step back and look at the picture that is being painted and what kind of life you would have if you followed the guidance of this voice. Play out the whole story.

BENEFITS Freedom, space, empowerment.

TIME Your inner critic can show up at any time, so be aware of it.

2

Take control

Now reclaim your future! Tell your inner critic what you think of that version of your life. You can be calm and loving, but if you have to get strong and real then go for it! Take control. Set the boundaries with your inner critic. When your inner critic feels tamed invite in your inner nurturer to congratulate you.

3

Reflect

Once you have given your inner nurturer the leadership position in your mind, take a moment of quiet to let it all settle and remember you can do this as many times as you need. Some inner critics respond to a gentle loving request to be quiet, but most need something a bit stronger.

Forgiveness is an important part of creating freedom from the past in your inner world and being open to the present. Forgiveness is the key part of many spiritual and compassion practices.

FORGIVENESS

You don't have to actively go and forgive everyone to their face – especially if seriously traumatic events have taken place. If you feel you can forgive the people that have harmed you by either writing a letter that you don't have to send them, or speaking to their souls in a meditation, this may be very freeing for you. It can also feel good to share it with them directly.

True forgiveness is not about the other person feeling better, but about you moving on from what has happened. If you don't feel ready to forgive somebody else, that's OK.

The most important person to keep forgiving is yourself. If you don't you can keep beating yourself up about both small and big things that are in the past now, and this prevents you from receiving new intuitive guidance and moving on. This can be as simple as saying each morning as part of your ritual, "I forgive myself."

There is a beautiful practice from the Polynesian Islands of the South Pacific, called Ho'oponopono, which means reconciliation and forgiveness. You don't have to direct this ritual at another person

– it's between you and the divine and ultimately it comes back to you. The original Ho'oponopono is a more extensive 14-step process that really clears karmic bonds. As a starting place, you can use this translated simple version.

Hold the vision of what you want to heal and repeat the words out loud or inside:

- I'm sorry
- Please forgive me
- Thank you
- I love you

BENEFITS Creates space, healing, courage.

TIME Forgive yourself on a daily basis, and others as often as you can. It only takes a moment.

CHANGE THE STORY

You can free yourself from replaying stories that keep you feeling small and limited by using this technique to change the story whenever you are triggered. This will bring your bodymind out of anxiety and back into a state of cohesion. The process improves intuitive capacity, stops energy drains, and opens you up into a state of clarity and intuition.

1

Breathe

Sit down in a comfortable position and close your eyes if this feels right to you. Breathe into and through your heart – feel your breath go in front of your heart through the back of your heart and out behind you.

BENEFITS
Re-centre, reclaim your energy.

TIME Spend 10 minutes on this.

2

Imagine

Bring a story into your mind where you were having fun, and felt safe, cared for, and free. You can have a few stories that you keep coming back to – that way you don't have to keep finding a new one in the moment whenever you're triggered.

3

Listen

Ask yourself what response would be empowered and most beneficial for your future? Listen for an answer, which may come in words or simply as a feeling. Write down what you experience or just sit with it and let it rise in your cells.

In Indian culture, astrology is a way of reading the map of the soul. From the information of your birth chart it is possible to see patterns, timings, and understand the general direction of your soul's path.

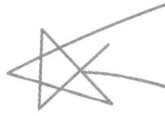

MAPS OF THE SOUL

We are each made unique, with our own personal destiny, which is why monoculture and comparison are so dangerous. Having your astrological birth chart read by either skilled Vedic or Western astrologers can provide a useful guide to life and your inner world. It can give you a sense of validation in understanding why your intuition has been leading you in a certain direction. This can also help to free you up from familial or societal expectations of your life, giving you permission to follow your inner guidance.

There are two newer processes that you can receive maps from; Human Design and the Gene Keys. Start by looking at your charts online, and then if you want to go deeper, the Gene Keys offers a course that takes you further. For Human Design you need a skilled practitioner to read your chart. It's remarkable how accurate these readings can be. These maps illuminate different aspects of your core being to help you understand the essence of your life and your true path more clearly.

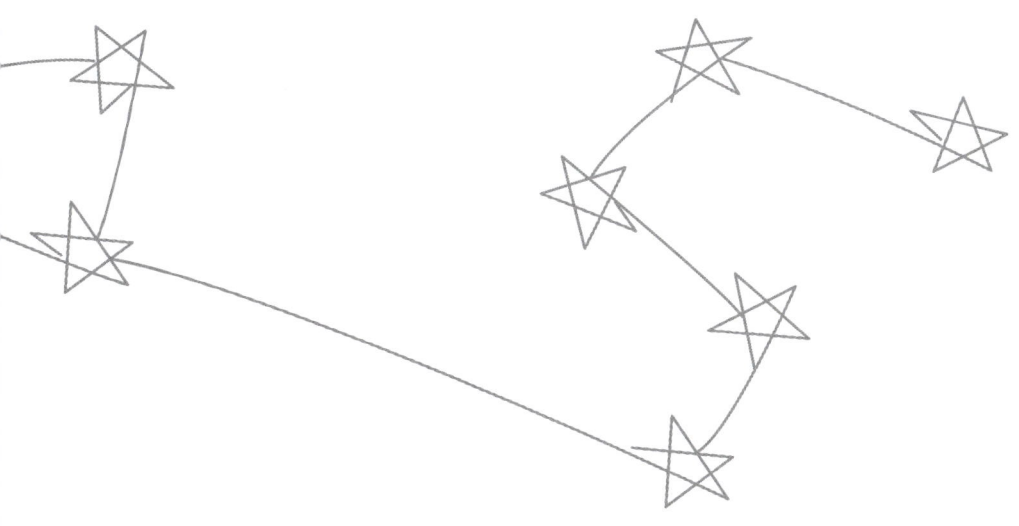

BENEFITS Attunes
your ego to your soul,
provides guidance.

TIME One reading
can last a lifetime,
or go whenever you
have big questions.

ASK YOUR INTUITIVE CHILD

As a child, you were intuitive. You knew who you were and why you were here; you were free – yet learning about how this world works. You would move from one game to another without needing to make a list of pros or cons. When you have a question, you can tap back into that free, innocent, loving, playful aspect of yourself and ask it.

1

Imagine

Close your eyes and take a few deep breaths. Imagine yourself as a child in a moment where you are happy and free. Connect to your innocence. Notice the colours, smells, and details of where you are.

BENEFITS
Reconnecting, know yourself.

TIME Make this a daily practice, observing your inner voices throughout the day.

2

Introduce

Introduce your present version
of yourself to the child version
of yourself; explain how it's nice
to see them and tell them that
you would love to ask them
a question.

3

Ask

Share your question and listen for
the wisdom offered. Write down
what you hear, for some of the
words might only come when you
start to write. Thank your
Intuitive Child.

HONOUR YOUR ANCESTORS

Indigenous traditions centre the importance of ancestors. More than anyone, your ancestors know what you are carrying into this life. Through connection with your ancestors you are able to bring through wisdom and intuitive guidance. Recognizing your lineage gives you perspective on where you have come from and offers a key to your freedom. Remember you are your ancestors' wildest dreams.

1

Offer

Make an offering to your ancestors – this could be placing some flowers or food on your altar, or lighting a candle. You might put photographs of your ancestors on your altar, or a talisman they passed down.

BENEFITS
Enhances self-knowledge and divine connection. Cultivates respect.

TIME You can spend 15 minutes on this or let it flow.

2

Connect

Close your eyes. Take deep breaths.
Connect to your own family and
spiritual lineage, if you have one.
Feel the presence of your ancestors.
Imagine them standing behind you
in their wisdom.

3

Listen

Ask your question. If you don't have
a specific question about your life,
you can simply ask for guidance.
Write down what you hear or listen
deep into your heart. Thank
your ancestors.

TALKING

For some of us, having space to talk with a good listener is the clearest way to hear our own intuition.

The act of simply talking something through out loud allows you to voice your feelings and desires in a way where you answer your own questions. As you listen and talk, maybe you will surprise yourself with the wisdom that comes out of your mouth.

For this level of interaction it's important to pick your friend well, and one-on-one is best to go deep. You want to talk to somebody who knows how to listen deeply, supports you from a place of care, and asks really good questions. Pick somebody that has an open and expansive nature – one who gives you space, and invites your full power with their presence.

A deep and meaningful with a good friend restores you to the beauty of your heart intelligence.

BENEFITS Free your wisdom from deep inside you.

TIME Take as long as you need, and engage in this as often as possible.

JOURNALING

Journaling is one of the simplest ways to listen to your intuition. When you write with a paper and pen you open up this special connection from your heart, through your arm and hand, to the page. The art of journaling is to let the words flow, and not worry about how they sound. Just start writing and even if the first part is total drivel, the good stuff will come. When you journal, let it be a space free from judgment. Let it flow, and then it becomes an important self-reflection tool. Here are three different ways that you can journal.

1

Free write

Pick up your notebook when you wake up or right before bed, with no particular theme or agenda other than to clear your head. Write without thinking, evaluating, or judgment. Just let the words flow onto the page and don't hold back or plan ahead. You might find when you read back what you wrote that you have laid out clear direction for yourself from your intuitive wisdom.

BENEFITS Clear guidance, self-awareness.

TIME This can be great as part of your morning practice, before bed or whenever the inspiration takes you.

2

Answers

When you are not sure what to do next or need to make a decision, pick up your notebook and pen and ask yourself a question. This could be as simple as "What do I need to know right now?" Or it might be a very specific question about something happening in your life. Don't use the word "should" but keep it open and high such as "Will this job allow me to live more in my purpose?"

3

Contemplation

A contemplation is a question that you sit with. You don't respond immediately but you let the answer come to you. Look at the question and then meditate on it. You can then journal with it. Get to know yourself better by tuning into a new question each week. Rather than assume you know the answer take the time to ask again, and allow a deeper wisdom to speak through you.

Your dreams are a prophetic part of your inner world. Through remembering your dreams you are able to notice signs, guidance, and the deep processing that happens when you sleep. You can bring these dreamworld insights into your day-to-day reality.

DREAM AWARENESS

Dreams offer a deep gateway into your subconscious. As your bodymind and ego go to sleep, your soul is unconstricted. As a starting point, set an intention to remember your dreams when you go to sleep. Learn to wake up without an alarm clock, so you awaken naturally and not mid-dream. Keep a notebook and pen next to your bed and in the morning, write down your dreams. Give each dream a title, and note down whatever you can remember or draw pictures. Don't judge your dreams, they work on a different reality to social norms.

Take time to honour the journey you have been on through the dreamworld and use your intuition to interpret any guidance you have received – such as a strong sense to call somebody who was in your dream, or a vision of something that is coming in your life or for all of us collectively. Through dreams you can learn the language of your soul and what it is revealing to you.

BENEFITS
Process subconscious,
receive guidance.

TIME Take a few minutes
before you sleep and as
soon as you wake up.

There is an intrinsic link between creativity and intuition; both take you beyond the realms of rational thought. If you become fully immersed in the present moment through a creative act, you enter into a state in which you can listen to your intuition. And best of all you don't need to be a skilled artist to reap the benefits – just indulge in the simple act of doodling.

DOODLING

1

Breathe

Take three deep breaths and remind yourself that there are no rules here. Don't think about the outcome; the act of doodling is natural, effortless, and focused on the now.

BENEFITS Connection; flow; quiet a busy mind; inspiration and new ideas; solutions and resolutions.

TIME Try 10 minutes or just go with the flow and let your page fill up.

2

Flow

Let your marks and drawings flow effortlessly onto the page with no judgment. Try to clear your mind as you allow your pen to move instinctively across the paper.

3

Reflect

When you have finished, take a look at your doodle. Does anything "speak" to you? How does it make you feel? Did any thoughts or feelings arise during your doodling?

TAROT & DIVINATION CARDS

The Tarot has been used since the eighteenth century as a divination tool. Through a reading you listen to what is happening in your inner world and what your higher self wants you to know. The reading gives you direction for the questions you hold and offers confirmation to your intuition.

BENEFITS Receive guidance, get some perspective.

TIME Pick one card daily, or spend an hour with a full reading when you have questions.

You can either go for tarot readings with a skilled reader, or work with your own cards. Choose the deck that you are drawn to – the original Tarot, or another themed deck such as Angel, Goddesses, or Spirit Animals. Each deck will come with information on the meaning of each card. Clear the energy in the cards before you start by holding the deck in your left hand and knocking on it with your right. You can start with a simple reading where you pick a card in the morning as guidance for your day, or ask a question and then pull a card. Sit with the card, reflect on it and how it makes you feel. Listen for any guidance. Or lay out three cards to represent past, present, and future to gain insights and support in making decisions that are aligned with your soul. The cards offer a sacred mirror in which your higher self brings to you the information that it wants you to see. Reading tarot offers you space for self-reflection and can be both playful and powerful, bringing information from your inner world into form.

PENDULUM

A pendulum can be helpful in getting confirmation of where your intuition was already guiding you, or as a way of listening to your inner wisdom. You can either buy a pendulum, or make one. If you make your own, put a stone onto a piece of string and ensure that the pendulum can swing freely in a circle without getting caught. The pendulum works with your body's electromagnetic field, and each one you work with will attune to your energy.

BENEFITS Gives you external validation, strengthens your connection with divine wisdom, helps you make decisions.

TIME Come to this whenever you need confirmation and guidance.

1

Centre yourself

For your pendulum to work accurately you need to be in a calm and connected state. Take a few deep breaths to centre yourself and welcome in grounding and protection energy.

4

"Yes" and "no"

Take away the hand that isn't holding the pendulum. Ask the pendulum "Show me yes" to see what movement it makes. Ask the pendulum "Show me no", and see what it does here.

2

Test movement

Pick up your pendulum with your non-dominant hand, holding the chain or string at the top with your thumb and index finger. Give it a little movement and check it can swing in circles or back and forth.

3

Your field

Hold the pendulum a few inches above your other hand, palm facing up to see what movement it naturally makes here. Then turn your hand over, palm down, to see what movement it makes now.

5

Practice

Now you can see how it shows you yes and no, ask it around 20 really simple questions – things that have very clear answers such as "Is my birthday in February?" or "Do I like chocolate?"

6

Ask questions

Now you can begin to ask questions about your life – avoid questions about predicting the future, or using the words "should" or "could". Ask clear questions such as "Is it in my highest to....?"

CONNECT WITH NATURE

The earth is our home, and we are a part of nature. We have become so domesticated that it is easy to forget this. We are wild beings. When we feel a connection to nature, it brings an aliveness to our souls, which opens up that connection with our intuition.

When you want to connect to the part of you that is bigger than you, that is the interconnectedness of our life on earth, take some time in nature. Maybe it's a long walk, sitting by a tree, looking up at the stars, swimming in the sea, even tending to your houseplants. Show up with care and presence. Be aware of being in a reciprocal relationship – where you are listening and giving, not just "extracting" connection for your social media, your creativity, or to feel better. Let your time in nature be that of true interbeing. Reconnect to your wild soul. A true experience of embodiment is in relationship with the earth.

BENEFITS
You remember that you are interconnected with this earth.

TIME This can be as simple as taking a moment to look up at the sky even if you are in a city, or could even be taking time off and emerging fully in the wilderness.

EARTHING

There is a simple practice of earthing, or grounding, that allows you to connect to the energy source that is in the earth. This is about bare feet and bare hands touching the ground, which reduces inflammation in your body. You absorb the negative electrons from the earth, which creates balance and supports your organ and cellular function. This re-charging restores you and opens up your direct connection to the earth's wisdom. If you can't get your bare feet on the ground, you can get earthing sheets and mats that link to the earth's energy through electricity sockets and bring you this connection.

BENEFITS Reduces pain, creates more energy, opens up direct relationship with the earth.

TIME Ideally a minimum of 30 minutes a day, but if not then as much as possible.

1

Step outside

Go outside into your garden, or if you don't have one, a nearby park or open space where there is earth – this could be either grass, sand, or mud.

2

Walk barefoot

Take off your shoes and socks and be barefoot on the ground. Walk around or lie on your back. If you feel it, place your hands on the earth too, or do some yoga asana poses.

3

Connect

Actively connect to the earth, asking for your inflammation and dis-ease to drain into the earth, and for a deeper sense of connection to the earth's wisdom.

4

Feel

Notice how it feels and what comes alive in your intuition. For you to be truly embodied, you also need to be embodied in your relationship to the earth.

There is a prayer central to the lives of the Native American Navaho people called The Beauty Way. How would it be to truly see life as beautiful?

THE BEAUTY WAY

Can you breathe into our interconnectedness in every moment as you walk this earth? Can you choose to honour the beauty that is present in both the challenging and joyous moments?

The Beauty Way is a whole approach to life – you live with a deep reverence for the sacred, for your inner world, others, and the earth. Live this as a way of being.

One way to embrace this way of life is to make offerings everywhere you go. Through these offerings, these sacred gifts, you are tuning into the fields of divine wisdom and intuition. You are asking for guidance and living in divine receptivity with the more-than -human world.

Your offering can be a song, a prayer, smiles, or a compliment. It can be food or flowers. You could pick up litter and leave places nicer than you found them. Your offerings can be doing something special for somebody or a random and anonymous act of kindness. Be creative in how you bring rituals of beauty into your life.

BENEFITS Appreciation of life, opening to wonder and synchronicity.

TIME Choose this as a way of life.

There are places in the world that are sacred sites where intuition comes alive as we connect to the alchemical transmission of the land.

PILGRIMAGES

Many people take pilgrimages to energy centres on the earth known as the earth's chakras, such as Mount Shasta in California (the root), Glastonbury in England (the heart), or Mount Kailash in the Himalayas (the crown). They could be locations along the earth's Ley Lines, or places of worship such as temples, mosques, or churches.

Pilgrimages could be into the wildness of nature, or to a town that has significance in your life, such as the place where your beloved grandmother lived. What makes this kind of visit a pilgrimage is that you go with the intention to expand your understanding of your Self, to deepen your connection with your intuition, and to listen deeply. Maybe it coincides with a time in your life when you are holding a specific question, or you have a threshold to honour. You don't always have to go far for your pilgrimage – you could take a day or an afternoon to go somewhere special with this desire to be in sacred connection, as you visit a tree you love, or a riverside. Be with your sense of curiosity and wonder, open to learning and unlearning; to being a living prayer.

BENEFITS Receive powerful transmissions and intuitive guidance.

TIME This could take anywhere from a few hours to the rest of your life.

All human beings are influenced greatly by the moon and astrology. This isn't the same as the type of astrology readings you find in magazines, or even the detailed charts read by experienced astrologers. There are general astrological happenings that affect everyone on earth.

LUNARSCOPES

The impacts of a particular planet being in retrograde or another set of planets being direct affects us all, often without us knowing anything about it. Much of our experience starts to feel less personal as we realize that all humans are being affected in similar ways. The same is true of the moon, which has a profound influence on us all. As we are 50 to 70 per cent water, in the same way we understand the moon affects the tides, so it affects the tides of our emotional being. When you have awareness of where we are in the moon cycle, and what astrological sign the moon is in, you can attune your life with these cycles rather than be raging against them, but not knowing why.

There is deep empowerment in living in tune with the cycles of life and recognizing that not every day or every week is the same. You'll find many great resources available online where lunarscopes are shared freely so you can always know where we are in the cycle. These often connect to your own intuitive sense of what is happening in the

collective, as well as how it is impacting you. As well as understanding where in the moon cycle we are, you can also learn where each planet is – what is direct and retrograde, and if we have an eclipse. All this information gives you an accurate picture of this moment. This knowledge and confirmation allows you to be more in tune with the deeper waves of humanity.

BENEFITS Live in tune with the cycles of life rather than resisting them.

TIME Spend an hour every two weeks understanding the astrology of this time.

NEW MOON RITUAL

The New Moon is a time of looking inwards and setting intentions. At this time, you cannot see the light of the moon, and the stars are visible in full glory. This is a moment to slow down, connect to your inner world, and let your intuition guide you into where you want to focus your energy on this next moon cycle.

3

Write

Open your eyes and begin to write your intentions. Start with "On this New Moon, with deep appreciation for all that I am, and all that I have, my intentions are..." Leave space in your intentions for surprises, so they cover how you want to feel and what you want to honour and focus on, not how it will all unfold.

BENEFITS
Stillness, reflection, quiet, intentions.

TIME 30 minutes (longer if desired); perform the ritual monthly, under the New Moon.

1

Prepare

Use this time as a portal into presence, holding past and future in your hands. Cleanse the space where you are holding the ritual in your own way. Make an altar with your selection of sacred objects. Light a candle and switch off the lights so you are sitting in the candlelight.

2

Contemplate

Complete a few rounds of alternate nostril breathing to bring balance and calmness. Ask yourself the contemplation question "What are my intentions for this New Moon?" Sit with the question in your meditation, lightly holding it and not forcing any answers to emerge. Let your intuition guide you.

4

Offer

Make an offering of your intention. Read it aloud, and then sing as a gift of your divine love. You could sing your favourite sacred songs, or chant mantras. Something beautiful happens when you bring out your voice. When you feel complete, snuff out the candle and give thanks.

5

Renew

Over this moon cycle, keep coming back to your intentions. If they are on your altar, you can read them every morning, or each night before bed. Stay in connection to these intentions. As you read them, embrace in a visceral way what these intentions feel like, as if you are already living them.

FULL MOON RITUAL

The Full Moon is a period of wild energy. We can experience at this time heightened emotions, desires, and mental processes. As we connect with each Full Moon, we develop our relationship with this energy to enhance our life. This is a time when we celebrate life and release all that no longer serves us.

BENEFITS Release; healing; cleansing; motivation and gratitude.

TIME 30 minutes (longer if desired); perform the ritual monthly, under a Full Moon.

1

Prepare

Select a space in the moonlight for your ritual. Bring your sacred objects together – this could just be a notebook and a candle, and/or other objects and offerings that you love. You may wish to leave these objects outside under the Full Moon to be cleansed and charged up.

4

Release

Write down a list of all you wish to release and how it has been holding you back from your freedom. Burn the paper in the flame of your candle to transform this energy into something else. If you can't burn it safely, put it in a bowl of water with salt and watch the words disappear.

2
Connect

Light your candle, then close your eyes, take three deep cleansing breaths, and allow yourself a few minutes to fully ground yourself in this moonlit moment. Find your centre and clear your mind by simply focusing on the sound of your breathing.

3
Contemplate

Notice how you are feeling as you sit and connect to this Full Moon. What is alive for you? Consider what it is you'd like to let go of in your life. What is no longer serving you? It may be an inner pattern, a project, an aspect of a relationship – or a combination of different things.

5
Celebrate

Celebrate this release and embody it through movement and dance. Let your body move freely and let go of any built-up stagnant energy and ways that these patterns or relationships have been holding tension in your body. If you feel it, free your voice with three howls.

6
Bathe

Sit or stand and look up at the moon, allowing yourself to bathe in its magnificence. Bring yourself into a place of deep gratitude for what you have in your life and the way everything is unfolding. Offer your gratitude to the moon silently or with words out loud. Snuff out your candle.

Plants are our greatest allies in the more-than-human world; they offer us guidance, healing, and can connect us to our psychic awareness.

PLANT MEDICINE

Plant medicine comes in many forms. It can be as simple as spending time communing with the trees, or the flowers, or your houseplants, befriending their spirits and understanding their healing properties. When you have a strong connection with your intuition, you open up all the realms of communication here. Plant medicine could be foraging for local superfoods hiding in plain sight as weeds, yet carrying many of the nutrients you need to be strong, healthy, and connected to the earth. It could mean preparing your food with deep love, gratitude, and devotion, eating plants that have a high energetic vibration as well as nutritional value. You could connect to the plants by drinking medicinal teas, or even through a tea ceremony.

You can work with plant medicines in the form of essential oils or flower essences, where certain plants or blends can open up specific qualities. For example, inhaling the scent of an essential oil can bring you into an almost immediate state of clarity, openness, and coherence. Having a high quality rose oil and frankincense oil to hand means you can always shift yourself to a higher vibration. Psychoactive plant medicines such as magic mushrooms or shamanic plants are being studied by leading institutions for their effects in healing trauma and connecting you to your intuition and soul, though they are currently illegal in most of the world.

BENEFITS Connect deeper with nature, healing, open intuition.

TIME Make a daily connection with plant medicine.

MUDRA

Mudra is a Sanskrit word that means seal or gesture. These hand mudras are part of yoga, and some are symbols of a connection to the divine. They affect our energy in the body circuitry, and create energetic seals for the flow of prana in the bodymind. In Ayurveda each finger represents a different element, and in some traditions a different planet. These gestures connect us more deeply to ourselves, to each other, and to the earth, opening our embodied intuition.

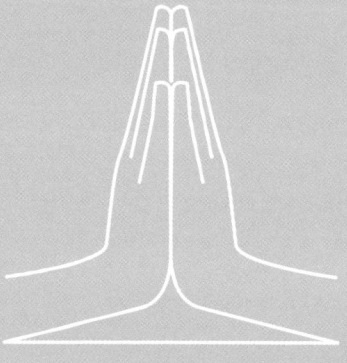

Anjali

Also known as prayer hands, this is where you bring your palms to touch in front of your heart. The word anjali means gift, prayer, or divine offering. Come into a space of humility and devotion with a gentle bow. Let there be even pressure between your fingers and leave a little bit of space between your palms. Soften your jaw.

BENEFITS Connection to yourself, connection to the divine.

TIME To feel the full effects of a mudra, hold it for at least seven minutes. Coming into a mudra even for a moment throughout your day will invite deeper connection.

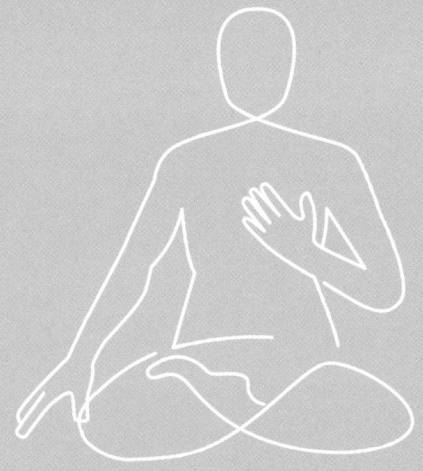

Bhumi Sparsha

This mudra connects you to yourself and to the earth. The name translates as "to lightly touch the earth". Place your left palm facing up in the centre of your lap, or a variation is to place this hand on your heart. Place your right hand on the ground with all fingers and your thumb touching the earth. Come into a state of honouring and blessing yourself and this earth.

Padma

Bring your hands together in anjali mudra. Gently move your middle three fingers out, so your hands are making a lotus flower, which is what the word padma means. Keep your thumb, little fingers, and base of your palms connected. In this mudra connect to your soul radiance, that essence of your true beauty and the abundant nature of your soul.

Mantra means sacred sound. In Sanskrit the word manas means mind, and also heart, and tra means protect. As a practice it has a way of quietening the default mode network in the analytical mind to open you up to connecting to the power of vibration and energy through which intuition speaks.

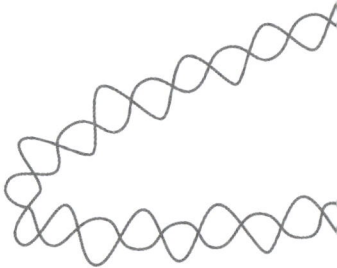

MANTRA

Through chanting mantras you bring healing shifts through the vibration of your own voice into the layers of your subtle body and physical body, and all the spaces in between. The most well known mantra is simply the sound Om, which is pronounced Aum. This is the primordial sound through which the whole universe vibrates. This sound connects you to the sacred hum of all life, to your inner teacher, and opens deep reverence. On a physical level, chanting mantras blocks stress chemicals, releases endorphins, and regulates your heart rate.

There are many mantras that you can learn such as the Gayatri mantra or mantras for different deity energies. You can chant these 108 times in a row by counting the beads on your japa mala. These sounds literally shift the information in every cell of your being.

Mantras are a part of many traditions. Any sounds or songs you make with this intention of deep connection and divine love become mantras. Playing mantras in your house can shift the energy that you feel there, transforming it into a sacred space.

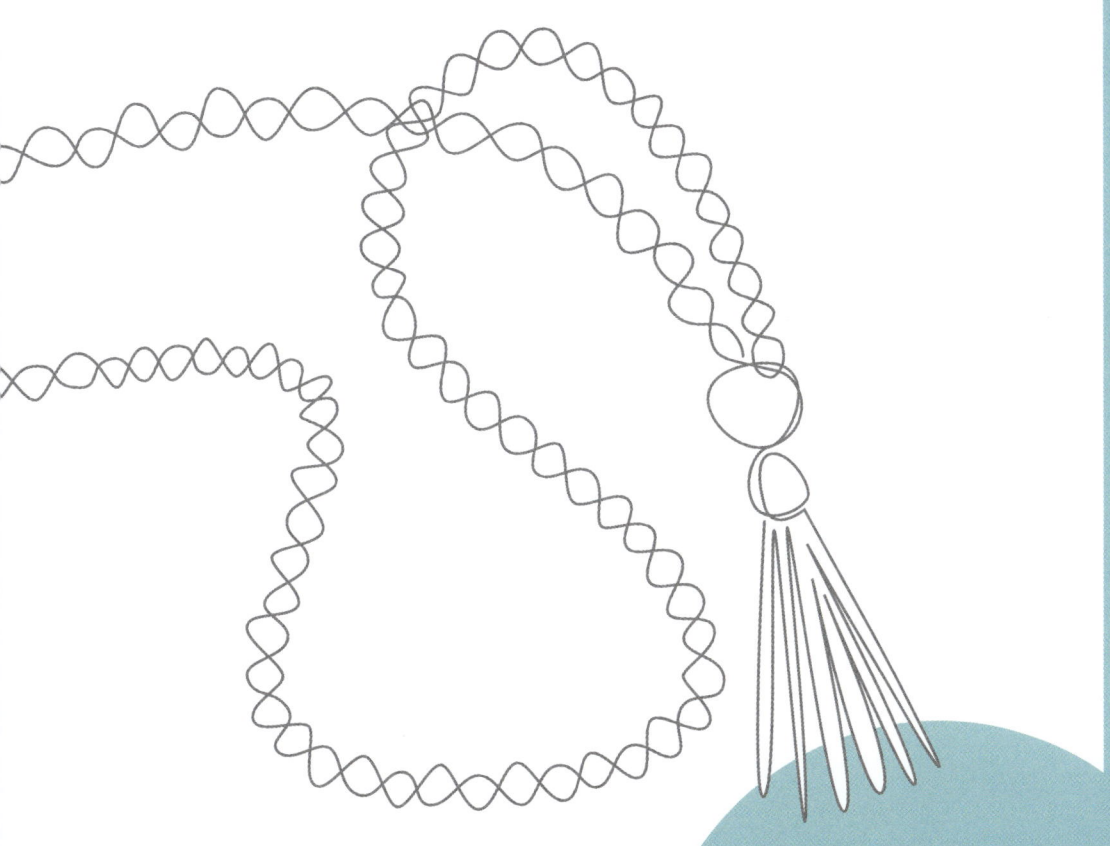

BENEFITS Clears your mind, recharges your spirit.

TIME You can immerse yourself in sacred sound as much as you desire.

FEEL THE EXPANSE

When we come to make a decision there are always many factors that we can consider. If we are making a decision centred on flow, we are feeling into the path of least resistance, into what feels the most light and expansive. This doesn't mean that it will be an easy outcome but that it will be in our highest divine path, which is where your intuition wants to take you.

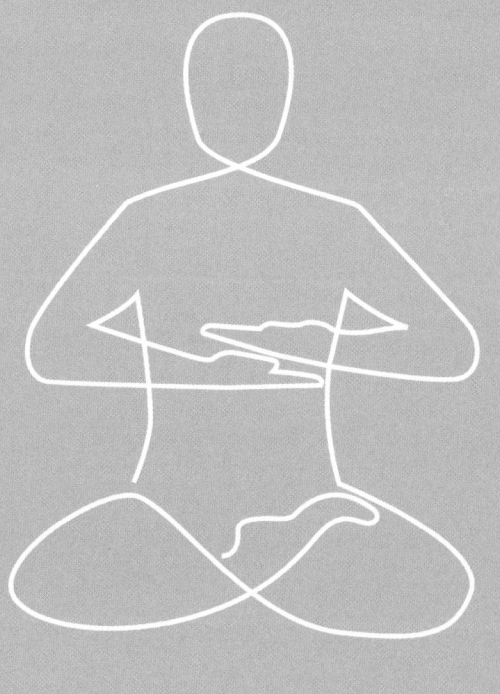

BENEFITS Make a decision in tune with flow and divine alignment.

TIME As you become attuned, this will take a few minutes.

1

Be still

Sit quietly in a meditation posture, and breathe into your heart. Connect to your space of heart intelligence. Remember there are no wrong decisions. Come up with two clear options. After you have worked with two, you can add in a third or fourth option. It's good to start simply.

2

First option

Place your hands in front of your heart, left hand resting in the right, palms facing up. Now feel this option, imagine that this is what you have chosen. Notice how it feels. What is the subtle energy like? Sit with it as long as you need to feel it. Focus on the feeling in your subtle body.

3

Second option

Let that one go and then come back into that still heart space. Take the other option and do the same thing as you did with the first. How does this one feel? You might not feel anything at first but the more you sit with it, the more you will activate this part of your consciousness.

4

Choose

Choose the one that feels the most expansive and light in its energy quality. You can bring in further options if neither feels right. If you can't feel a big difference or they feel the same come back to this later or another day. Remember everything is always moving.

Synchronicities and signs are wonderful feedback loops we get that show us we are in flow. This can be as simple as somebody being in your dream and then the next day they call when you haven't spoken for years, or wanting to start dating again and then being set up on a blind date.

LOOK FOR SYNCHRONICITIES

Looking for synchronicities and making a note of them is a powerful way of inviting more flow into your life, and bringing your attention to where flow is unfolding.

You can also ask for a sign, such as "If this is the true next step for me, show me a yellow car within the next 24 hours." It helps to make your signs not too obscure so they are impossible, or so common that they are everywhere, such as a pigeon in a city. Be open for where signs might show up in unusual places – for instance, you might ask for a hippo, and then see a sticker of one on a child's backpack.

Open yourself up to be in this sense of wonder and in a reciprocal relationship with life as it is happening. Let your intuition guide you, and notice and enjoy what is showing up.

BENEFITS
Delightful, provides confirmation.

TIME Let this become part of how you experience life.

VISIONING YOUR FUTURE

One way to activate your intuition and open up into flow consciousness is to spend time in creative visualization. This is a practice that can support your healing by, for example, seeing yourself healed of a physical condition or feeling whole again after losing someone you love. You could also use it to feel yourself fully embodying your intuitive gifts. You are powerful – use this wisely.

3

Visualize

Move your attention to another screen that is towards your left, so your eyes are now looking up and left. On this screen visualize your near future, where some steps have been taken and everything is feeling easier or you are closer to your goals. Pay attention to how it feels.

BENEFITS Creating an opening of possibility for your visions to come into form.

TIME Give yourself at least 20 minutes, let it be spacious.

1

Connect

Sit up in a meditative posture and come into the space of your heart. Relax and connect to the beauty of your life. Breathe into this place and then bring your attention up into your third eye. With your eyes closed, look up imagining a screen in the space of your third eye.

2

Paint a picture

Create a picture of the present on the screen – how does it feel? Exaggerate the pains and difficulties you have going on in your life right now to their worst moments so you can allow the reality of what you are experiencing to be felt.

4

Dream

Now move your vision further to the left, where you may even feel uncomfortable as you are not used to looking this far up and to the left. On this screen, paint the picture of your full vision. Remember to engage all the senses and don't hold back. Don't censor your vision; let it come to life.

5

Surrender

Bring your awareness back to your heart and to the present moment. Connect to your gratitude and surrender this vision. By allowing yourself to sit and come into a state of visioning you open the gateways to bring into being whatever your highest guides you towards.

THE LIBRARY

This beautiful visualization takes you into a state of flow in your inner world. Activate your intuitive compass to let go of what no longer serves you and pull in the resources that you need. This requires being able to centre into your inner world and stay with the visualization, which without an audio to guide you is a skill in itself but so possible if you are a practised meditator or you have a very visual inner world.

BENEFITS Allows a deep clearing of your inner world, and helps you bring what you need into it.

TIME Give yourself at least 15 minutes.

1

Prepare

Find a quiet space where you won't be interrupted and sit in a meditative posture, or lie down in a comfortable restorative position if you can do so without falling asleep. Close your eyes. Take some deep breaths in stillness to silence your mind and come into a receptive space.

4

Release

Take the trolley out to the garden where there is a fire pit burning. Take each book one by one, look at the title and then release this quality within yourself as you throw the book into the fire. Feel yourself letting go of all these qualities that no longer serve you.

2

Your library

Go into a beautiful, peaceful garden in your inner world. Find the gate and open it, then walk towards the door that you see. Take the key from around your neck, and open the door. You are now in your own library; the perfect space for your creativity and intuition to flourish.

3

Your books

This library represents your inner world, and here you find all the books that you are storing. For example, you might have one called Lack of Confidence or Cynicism. You find a hand-crafted trolley. Intuitively, you pick up all the books you no longer need and put them inside it.

5

Receive

Now take your trolley to the other gate at the end of the garden, and open it. Here you find a bustling market. Walk around, see what catches your attention, and put it in your trolley. If any of the people here give or offer you anything, receive it and place it in your trolley.

6

Savour

When you feel you have what you need, go back to your garden and into the library. Lay out your gifts. Savour each one and find a place for it in this library, your sacred space. When you are ready, step back into the garden. Ground this experience into your body, and open your eyes.

INTUITION DIARY

When you are really focused on creating trust in your intuition, it is helpful to keep an intuition diary. Here you can keep track of the intuitive insights you had for yourself and what happened when you listened to them – or when you chose not to.

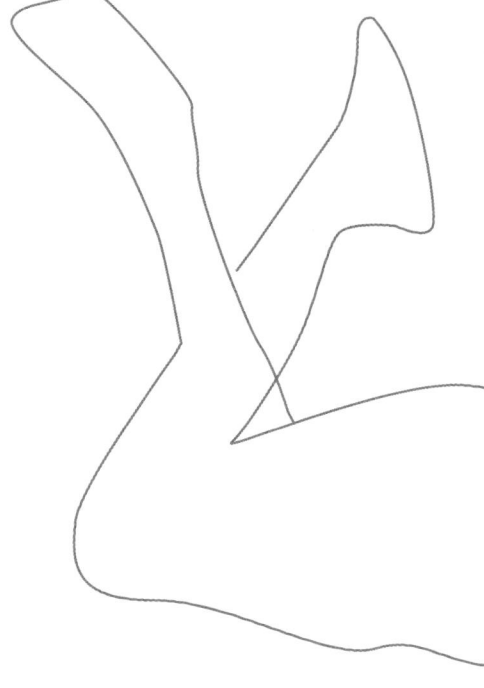

This way you can learn from the past. For example, you got a clear intuition not to take on a certain project, but you did it anyway and you ended up getting ill. Or something smaller – you had an intuition to not take your usual route, did so anyway, and ended up in traffic. Becoming really aware of the consequences of not listening is really important as through this you can grow trust. You begin to see what the stakes are.

Likewise, write down the moments that you listened to your intuition, and how it unfolded – what did it feel like? What did it open up to? What did you learn? Write the stories with as much detail as you can.

Write about how you received the intuition – how did it feel in your body? How did you get this sense of knowing? Let this diary be a way of bringing the unseen into the seen, of making your intuition a very real and important part of your life.

BENEFITS Gives you a measure of what is unfolding.

TIME Come to this daily for as long as you need.

TEST YOUR HUNCHES

This playful practice gives you space to explore and test your intuition, opening up your psychic awareness. Have fun with this as you make a note of the hunches that you have about how things will play out around you. These hunches can be about anything you can imagine, such as when you meet a friend's new partner how long you intuit they will be together, or if meeting a friend what colour you intuit they will be wearing. By writing these down, you get to test yourself and can also notice what helps you be in tune or when you might miss something.

BENEFITS
Deepens trust, opens psychic awareness.

TIME Try this at least once a week.

1

Note it down

Have a notebook or a note on your phone where you write down your hunches. Any little hits you get, make a note of them. You can also add how you are feeling so you get a sense of what makes you most in tune.

2

Feel it

Experiment with both hunches that just come to you, and ones that you "look for" by closing your eyes and feeling into it. The more you practise feeling in this way, the more attuned you will become.

3

Assess

Keep coming back to your notes to see which ones came into reality. Make a note of which ones happened as you saw. Don't beat yourself up if you get anything wrong – it's play and practice.

4

Re-assess

Remember that the future isn't written, so your intuitive hit might have been right in that moment, but things change. You can update your hunches as they evolve based on the information as it is changing.

GRATITUDE

Gratitude is the practice that holds trust at the centre of life. When you live in gratitude you are peaceful, content, awake. You are embodying your intuition and inviting in possibility. You are present. You are free. You give yourself permission to be in heartfulness, the space of gratitude, and your whole body feels it. In this physical vibration you open your life up to receive and share more beauty. When you attune your bodymind to the vibration of gratitude, without thought or word, you can feel it through your breath. It brings a sacred aliveness to the moment.

1

Align

Deeply inhale into your heart, drawing the breath all the way to the back of your heart. Become aware of the earth underneath you and the cosmos above you as you feel your presence in time and space. Through your breath and your attention, bring yourself into a state of alignment.

BENEFITS Presence, trust, divine connection.

TIME Come to this as often as you remember in a day. It will change your life.

186

2

Acknowledge

Say either in your mind or speak out loud three things, big or small, for which you are grateful in this moment. Or if you prefer, write them down. If you are not alone, involve those around you, such as sharing them with your kids at bedtime or with your partner as you wake up.

3

Assimilate

Let the vibrations of gratitude pour through every cell of your being. Notice how focusing on that for which you are grateful brings joy, grace, and humility into your bodymind. Throughout your day bring your focus back to gratitude. Let the beauty of this life flow through you.

INDEX

Index entries in **bold** refer to practices.

SOURCES

11 B. Kasanoff, *Intuition Is The Highest Form Of Intelligence?*, Forbes [online], 21 February 2017, accessed June 2020. https://www.forbes.com/sites/brucekasanoff/2017/02/21/intuition-is-the-highest-form-of-intelligence/#4a1a97c63860

12 C. Myss, *The Three Levels of Intuition, from Advanced Energy Anatomy*, Sounds True Inc, 2001.

M. Pigliucci, *Answers for Aristotle*, Basic Books, 2012.

18 J. Neal, *Edgewalkers: People and Organizations That Take Risks, Build Bridges, and Break New Ground*, Praeger, 2000.

30–33 B. H. Lipton, *The Biology of Belief: Unleashing the Power of Consciousness, Matter & Miracles*, Hay House, 2015.

32 J. Dispenza, *Becoming Supernatural*, Hay House, 2017.

35–39 B. van der Kolk, *The Body Keeps the Score: Mind, Brain and Body in the Transformation of Trauma*, Penguin, 2015.

G. Maté, *When the Body Says No: The Cost of Hidden Stress*, Vermillion, 2019.

HeartMath Institute, *Science of the Heart: Exploring the Role of the Heart in Human Performance, Chapter 7 Intuition Research: Coherence and the Surprising Role of the Heart*, HeartMath Institute [online], accessed June 2020. https://www.heartmath.org/research/science-of-the-heart/intuition-research/

Your third brain: The microbiome, Immortalis [online], accessed June 2020. https://immortal.is/

J. Wolkin, *Meet Your Second Brain: The Gut*, Mindful [online], 14 August 2015, accessed June 2020. https://www.mindful.org/meet-your-second-brain-the-gut/

John Hopkins Medicine, *The Brain-Gut Connection*, John Hopkins Medicine [online], accessed June 2020. https://www.hopkinsmedicine.org/health/wellness-and-prevention/the-brain-gut-connection

P. A. Levine, *Waking The Tiger: Healing Trauma*, North Atlantic Books, 1997.

T. Judelle, *Tara Judelle on Embodied Flow, Transformational Yoga and The BodyMind*, The Future is Beautiful with Amisha Ghadiali, E82.

41–45 J. Dispenza, *Becoming Supernatural*, Hay House, 2017.

63 M. Emoto, *The Hidden Messages in Water*, Pocket Books, 2005.

65–69 C. Wallis, *Near Enemy #3: Listen to your heart*, Hareesh [online], 15 August 2017, accessed June 2020. https://hareesh.org/blog/2017/8/15/near-enemy-3-listen-to-your-heart#

J. Faerman, *Mapping The Evolution Of Consciousness: A Holistic Framework For Psychospiritual Development*, Flow Conscious Institute, 2016.

J. Neal, *Edgewalkers: People and Organizations That Take Risks, Build Bridges, and Break New Ground*, Praeger, 2000.

73–74 S. Kempton, *Inner Revolution*, Center for Integral Wisdom [online], 19 August 2009, accessed June 2020. https://www.ievolve.org/inner-revolution-sally-kempton/

ABOUT THE AUTHOR

AMISHA GHADIALI is an intuitive therapist and a yoga and meditation teacher. She is the host and founder of the globally acclaimed podcast The Future Is Beautiful. Interested in where our inner and outer worlds dance, the podcast weaves together politics, spirituality, creativity, and sustainability – to inspire us each to rise up, move beyond silos, and co-create a Beautiful Future. As a facilitator, Amisha has a gift of bringing people into connection with themselves, each other, and the earth. She hosts retreats, workshops, and rituals around the world. In addition, she works one-to-one with private sessions and her Presence Leadership Mentoring programme, which assists the transforming of unconscious patterning, opening up new qualities within, and anchoring daily practice and rituals which support a lifestyle that recognizes the sacred, the importance of intuition, and inspires embodiment of what this time calls forth in us. She hosts an online membership community called Presence: for Creative, Connected and Courageous Living. Her own training has included energy medicine, priestess initiation, yoga teaching, meditation, and deep time learning with mystics, teachers, swamis, and nature. This is combined with a background in politics, social enterprise, and sustainable fashion including her own jewellery label with the tagline, "elegance rebellion".

Go to www.amisha.co.uk for more information and extra guidance.

ACKNOWLEDGMENTS

I dedicate this book to the memory of my father, Dr Himanshu Ghadiali, who left his body while I was writing this. He lived his life by his intuition and taught me to do the same. He was visionary, courageous, and wise. I honour his liberation with so much love. Both he and my delightful mother, Dr Hema Ghadiali, have supported me unconditionally in forging my own path in life, taking risks, and knowing my true self. And for that I am eternally grateful. I offer gratitude to all our ancestors in their wisdom who support from the other side, naming my Jain grandparents Kokila & Nautambhai Ghadiali and my Hindu ones, Tara & Jhinabhai Desai – and to the future generations for the codes they are bringing into this world, naming my beautiful nieces Yume-Tara Rose and Kora Yasmin Sawaswati.

Thank you to my dear teacher Sally Kempton who has been an incredible support, always reflecting back to me my Shakti. Thank you to my wonderful friends who have been so present and encouraging, especially Robin Dhara, Amy Daneel, Mischa Varmuza, and Tess Amodeo Vickery. Thank you to Izzy Winkler and Tilia treehouse at West Lexham, Norfolk (where much of this book was written). Thank you to all my teachers, from the rivers to the trees, and the many humans I have studied with. Thank you Sianna Sherman, Jyoti, and Justin Faerman. And deep gratitude to all the wisdom keepers, wise women and holy men in every culture who have risked their lives to protect and share sacred knowledge, so that we may embody it now.

Thank you to the whole team at DK for their beautiful work and for trusting me, especially Dawn Henderson for her vision and Emma Hill for her patience, dedication, and making the process joyful, even in a global quarantine. And lastly, thank you to you for bringing your intuition into this world. May these studies of my intuition be in service to the full realization of your own.